The
# Findhorn
Book of

# Unconditional Love

*by*

Tony Mitton

First published by Findhorn Press 2003

ISBN 1 84409 006 X



British Library Cataloguing-in-Publication Data.
A catalogue record for this book is available from
the British Library.

Edited by Shari Mueller
Cover and internal book design by Thierry Bogliolo
Cover background photograph by Digital Vision
Cover central photograph by Creatas/Dynamic Graphics

Printed and bound by WS Bookwell, Finland

Published by
**Findhorn Press**
305a The Park, Findhorn
Forres IV36 3TE
Scotland, UK

tel 01309 690582
fax 01309 690036
e-mail: info@findhornpress.com

**findhornpress.com**

# TABLE OF CONTENTS

## ACKNOWLEDGEMENTS



Quotations from The Holy Bible are taken from the Authorised (King James) Version.

Many friends have given me their unconditional love. I have learned from them and this book is really theirs, but it would be invidious to name them. They know who they are. However, I will name four: Karin Bogliolo, my publisher, who conceived the idea; my wife Kathy who has loved me, sustained me and mostly forgiven me throughout the gestation; Thierry, Karin's husband, who has done creative work in the delivery room; and the Beloved, who is our Guide and our Source. To those too who have contributed to the book and to all, I give my grateful thanks.

# PROLOGUE

This book is about unconditional love as I have learned it since living in the Findhorn Community. The name Findhorn properly belongs to the ancient fishing village where the community was born, but in these pages I shall use it for the community itself. It is a spiritual community without dogma or guru, where each person learns his or her own way to best serve the planet in unconditional love. At Findhorn people can belong to any faith or none, and no one will try to convert them. All that matters is the desire to serve and make your individual contribution. Then you fit right in.

The Findhorn experience is a personal one, giving to each of us what we need for our growth and spiritual advancement, so this book must be personal too. If it is personal, can it deal comprehensively with all the issues, practices, conceits and misconceptions surrounding unconditional love? Probably not, but what is presented will be authenticated by experience. It was part of life at Findhorn that when we were tackling some personal issue and thought we were on our own, we found, talking about it to our friends or in departmental meetings, that many others in the community were dealing with the same challenges. This synchronicity suggested that we were actually developing a group consciousness, which was one of our objectives and which served us very well in the various projects we created and enjoyed. So, when starting this book, it seemed logical that I should form a group to participate in it. Mainly, they comprise my closest family and friends whose experiences illumine the nature of unconditional love; their contributions are included in these pages. Some wish to be identified and some do not, but in all cases I have made clear that the authorship is different.

Having no dogma or guru, Findhorn draws on whatever resource brings holistic health and healing to our planet. In no way should this book be seen as representing Findhorn's teaching on Unconditional Love. There is no such teaching, only an attitude. A bibliography, attached at the end, lists the major works that, in a general sense, I have found useful. Some of them are sublime and I think it important, when reading, to let the heart do the thinking. In that way we may get to the core of the author's experience.

One never really leaves Findhorn and we are all part of a world community, so it is my hope that many of our experiences may have been experiences that you, the reader, have had too. Writing this book has been a learning process for me, and I have to come to recognise fragments and moments of unconditional love in myself as I have worked through the material. I hope that you may do so too, and that with open hearts we may realise that Humanity is One Soul, whom we can love unconditionally in each one of us. In that spirit I dedicate this book to you.

Tallahassee, Florida,
September 2002

*PART ONE*

# ORGANISING THE GARDEN

Renata loved the wild garden around her home. It overlooked a great lake with views of high mountains beyond, and contained entrancing vistas of flowering shrubs, evergreens and fruit trees that hid small moments of delightful colour and contrast, all set amid a meadow of wild flowers and a few formal beds. The garden possessed a powerful life and was a playground for the nature spirits who made it their own. Then Renata fell in love with Peter and brought him to the garden. He became very quiet.

"How do you like it? Don't you feel the atmosphere?" she asked.

"Well, I see all that needs doing," said Peter.

*[Renata's account, summarised from* In Perfect Timing *by Peter Caddy]*

# 1. MOP AND BUCKET

"Unconditional love? I don't believe it exists."
"That depends on your level of consciousness."
*[Overheard in conversation]*

Romantics speak of the garden of love, and if that's what it is, it's a wild garden, a riot of competing claims and affections. So let us use this first section to bring a bit of order to it, so we can see both the wood and the trees. The need for love is a fundamental human trait, but when I was a young man, no one spoke of unconditional love. Actually, in my particular circle, one would have been thought a sissy (ancient term for wimp). We might speak of Gandhi in terms of non-violence, or a minister might speak of Jesus as personifying forgiveness, but unconditional love? Would such a term not mean the giving of love without expectation of return? Romance novels may portray such a thing as possible but never as desirable.

I don't think that the romance novels are talking about unconditional love at all. For them, love always contains a notion of end-gaining – possession of the beloved – who then becomes an object. Unconditional love has no goal in view. It simply is. It is the love that made us. This is true whether we see our beginning as happening through the sexual act, that instant when all thought is lost, even of the other, and you know only the ecstasy of the moment; or whether we see ourselves as the product of God's creation. If we return the love that conceived us, whether to our mother or our God, we ground unconditional love in the core of our being.

Our need for love is not, fundamentally, a need for the perfect sweetheart, wife or lover, but for the unconditional love that lives in the essence of our being and is God's love that created us, or, if you are an atheist, the love inherent in sexual union. I believe that this is the root of humankind's restlessness, that we are looking for unconditional love and do not realise that it is already within us. So we fantasise and when we hear about unconditional love, we think we must emulate God and extend it to everybody immediately.

Then, of course, we flunk and feel a failure. Indeed, I think unconditional love is a universal principle, but it is also a learning experience: we draw a little bit of it from our core and give it to a husband, wife, lover, friend or pet, thus grounding unconditional love in our personality. If we take the conscious decision to choose love as our spiritual practice, our personality blooms and flourishes. We grow. In this lies the secret of happiness, steadfast and complete, self-affirming and generous, as far removed from ordinary happiness as unconditional love is from ordinary loving. How to make this experience our constant companion is the purpose of this book.

There is a school of thought that holds that God is above having attributes. Others think differently. Islam speaks of "Allah of the ninety-nine qualities." Christianity speaks of God as Love, though it adds Power and Glory as an afterthought. Inconveniently, the Church's familiar themes of God's Justice, Day of Judgement, Heaven or Hell, contradict the idea of unconditional love, so I must also address these teachings, which make unconditional loving hard. For myself, I think of Love as a Divine Principle and therefore Absolute, extending everywhere. This means that no shadow of hatred or condemnation can enter the mind of the Most High.

We are usually averse to new ideas unless they are embodied in a gadget or a new car. We raise objections, or make the thing appear more difficult than it really is. Could we unconditionally love a serial killer? That's not the question. Rather, the question is about the people we know personally. For example, can we love our children unconditionally? The answer is probably 'yes', qualified when we remember their little teen-age traits, some of which will have continued into adulthood. Qualifications don't make for unconditional love, but we know that there is a part somewhere in us, and somewhere in that child, where we can love and be loved unconditionally for ever and always. And do you remember falling in love? That crazy state when you were totally filled with the other, knowing bliss and living it, never mind that later on the dogs of life ate part of your dinner.

Children and lovers are easy, you may say. Try someone a little harder. For that I'll have to delve into my own experience and ask you to track along with me. I'll start with Peter Caddy, co-founder of the Findhorn Community. This is a spiritual centre in north-eastern Scotland which encourages people to come to learn how best they may use their unique gifts to serve the planet in unconditional love. The three people associated with its founding are Peter Caddy, Eileen Caddy and Dorothy Maclean. It achieved fame in its infancy by growing amazingly large and succulent vegetables on barren, sandy soil, the result of some rather light-hearted co-operation with the angelic spirits overlighting plant species. At that time they were desperately poor and needed the garden produce for subsistence.

Since about 1970 Findhorn has been growing people. Those living there can be of any religion or no religion. There is no guru, and though people pay for the courses they attend, no one asks you to put all your money into the common pot. There are two rules – no smoking in public places, and no illegal drugs anywhere. Findhorn is both the Foundation, a legal entity that holds the property, organises education and pays its staff, and the Community, which is a much looser aggregation of people who live in the surrounding area, work in conventional pursuits and broadly embrace Findhorn's principles and practice. As of 2002, about 200 people work in the Foundation and 1,000 in the neighbouring Community, but there are many more thousands that form a community world-wide.

Peter used to tell the story of the new student at Pythagoras' mystery school. On his way to his first early morning class, this student encountered a pile of dust and rubbish in the corridor. He wondered what sort of school this was, which failed to clean up such an obvious mess. The next day the trash pile was still there, and the day after that, and this continued till he left in disgust, muttering that he could not remain in a place that did not clean up its rubbish. He had never noticed the mop and bucket standing against the corridor wall.

If I am to write about unconditional love, I'll have to pick up my mop and bucket. And since I've been talking about him, I'll go to work on Peter Caddy. Most people got on very well with him but my relationship was uneasy, for reasons I didn't clearly understand. Can I give him unconditional love nonetheless? Not many of you will have known him, so let me give you an image to work with. He was like a CEO, a man of action and always gung-ho to get started, often based on his personal intuition. On the other hand he had very little ego, for his ideal was planetary service, not profit. He could be dogmatic and dictatorial, but if you took him to task with well-argued criticism, he would listen and change the plans he was making. Yet I found myself disliking his grandiosity; his apparent lack of compassion and empathy, particularly in respect of children who were my particular focus; and more especially his betrayal of his wife Eileen whom I unashamedly worship. It will surely be easier to love him unconditionally if I focus on his virtues. His enormous achievements; his energy; his joy; his intuition; his sense of God's divine plan for humanity; his willingness to carry out his part of it at whatever personal cost; his mastery; his ability to dismiss mistakes – "That was God's way of testing me" – and go beyond them; this list could go on. I am told too that in his later life, particularly with his last wife Renata, when his great tasks were completed and he was free to open up and be himself, he became quite a different person. But I still ask, is a catalogue of virtues enough for one person to love another unconditionally?

Is it true that if I can't forgive, I can't love? I find that Peter's desertion of Eileen sticks in my gullet. Which leads me to own one of my own traits, good in itself but tending to excess. It is the need to protect others. Why do I need to forgive Peter for his dealings with Eileen, when Eileen has already forgiven him and acknowledged that all their interactions were necessary for their joint spiritual growth? In plain language, it's no business of mine. However, it was an offence against accepted social mores. And this is where people most often get stuck, saying, "I can't forgive X for the way he/she treated Y," when what they are really saying is, "That behaviour makes me feel threatened." Viewed from this angle, the threat becomes manageable and forgiveness possible.

It may be that the behaviour threatens not so much oneself as one's investment in a stable society. Or the behaviour may affect one more personally, either as a fear that one may be tempted to act likewise, or be a victim. In either case it causes us to reassess our relationships. Is this a bad thing?

Rather it is a useful challenge, making us examine what could be improved, communicate ideas and avoid getting into ruts. And on the way we can forgive ourselves for disliking change so much. The ability to laugh at ourselves is quite invaluable. And you know what? Laughter often leads to loving.

People say that we must love ourselves before we can love others. Loving ourselves may be one of our hardest tasks. It doesn't help being virtuous, even if we are religious. There's a saying in the Church that the greatest saint is the greatest sinner, meaning that as a person's awareness of God grows, so does awareness of their sinfulness. So that's not the road to go. The unconditional lover must be a happy person. We think of love as an emotion, but unconditional love is really a decision, taken in the heart. In the next chapter we'll look at the different ways of loving and get a clearer idea of what unconditional love really means. First, please help me by doing this preparatory exercise to flex the soul's heart muscles.

*Exercise*

*Think of the person in your life whom you love the most. They may be relative or friend, living or dead. Think of the traits that endeared them to you. Then go beyond those, and think just of the person and how you love them. Stay there for a while, then release them with your blessing and return to present time.*

# 2. DIFFERENT LOVINGS

"There are worse occupations in this world
than feeling a woman's pulse"

*[Laurence Stern]*

David Spangler is an unassuming individual with a penetrating mind and spiritual insight. He came to Findhorn in 1970 and for several years was Peter

Caddy's right hand man. While at Findhorn he received a series of communications from a lofty Being known as Limitless Love and Truth, affectionately dubbed LLT by community members. The conjunction of these two principles, love and truth, is all-important, for one without the other can go overboard and destroy the human being. When I was at Findhorn, we usually wished each other "Love and Light" – meaning the Light of Truth – when we bade farewell. If we are going to foster our capacity for unconditional love, we must bring the light of truth along with us. David Spangler's contribution will help us do that.

In a manuscript in progress, presented to an online class in Incarnation Spirituality, David tells of a time at Findhorn when he was sitting in on a group and a young man entered the room. He had just returned to the community after living 'in the real world', and everyone greeted him warmly. As he sat down, he said feelingly, "It's good to be back in a place where I can't be fired!" To quote David: "To me, this summed up a lot of what I felt then was wrong with Findhorn, mainly the abdication of responsibility, and unconditional acceptance and love gone wonkers (ancient esoteric term…)." It is an example of how unconditional love can be misunderstood, as a belief that somehow we are not to be held accountable for our behaviour.

The need for unconditional acceptance seems quite widespread, particularly among those with a tendency to be irresponsible. I used to work for a Department of Corrections in the United States and once had occasion to address a group of women prisoners on work release. I wanted to give them a picture of a type of life that was different from the soul-destroying round of minimum wage and crowded, drug addicted neighbourhoods that most could expect when they finally went home. I spoke of the possibility of making a community where everyone pitched in to do the jobs that needed doing, whether it was earning money or cleaning dishes – sharing and caring. Challenged whether such a place existed on this earth, I spoke of Findhorn. Immediately my audience saw the place as Shangri-la, where the most labour demanded would be to pluck fruit that ripened on the trees. My warnings that drugs were not tolerated went unheeded. That's what 'they' said about prison, haha! I could see some of them figuring how much a plane ticket might cost, and how they could get the money.

Actually, Findhorn once had this very same problem. In its early days, as word of the community spread around, it became a magnet for hippies. Peter, who had been a squadron leader in the wartime Royal Air Force, had a drastically simple solution: "Clean yourself up and work – or leave!"

David Spangler's manuscript tells how unconditional love can be disempowering and weaken a person's capacity for self-sovereignty. It can foster dependency and co-dependency in the relationship:

"For some people, I think, unconditional love is a way of avoiding the complications and conditions of selfness. If I surrender or ignore my boundaries, then I don't have to worry about or do the hard work of maintaining them. Boundaries don't have to be separative at all; they are defining, and they help coalesce and focus energy and presence in a unique way. There is a world of difference between being unique and different, and being separative and isolating.

"I have certainly met people who seem to me to love unconditionally...But in my experience such people are also powerful individuals. They have not lost anything in themselves by loving unconditionally. It's not that they don't have boundaries; it's rather that their boundaries are very inclusive and interactive."

Unconditional love does not say, "I love everyone equally," but rather, "I love everyone appropriately and in response to their uniqueness." Unconditional love does not mean unconditional acceptance of behaviours.

When I think of how I love my children, David seems to be spot on. I love them appropriately. But I know that there is also a space where we love each other unconditionally. Where to go look for it? And would David agree with my earlier proposition that falling in love may be like loving unconditionally? I think he would be suspicious, because when we fall in love, we surrender boundaries. I wonder whether it's then Life that is coursing through us, just masquerading as Love for its own procreative purposes. That's when we regress to be the immature child suckling at the breast of the Great Mother. A heretical proposition, I know, but think about it! There is a ton of difference between loving and falling in love. Most of us have experienced both. When we fall out of love but continue loving, we may hope to progress to David's more mature 'appropriate love' and then go beyond to loving unconditionally.

Before continuing this discussion, I feel the need to distinguish appropriate love from the more transactional type, the "I'll love you if you cook my dinner every night" syndrome. In appropriate love, we don't ask our partner to adjust to us, nor do we need to adjust to them. Each of us keeps our sovereignty, and we share whatever space our distinct sovereignties allow. If this proposition reduces the incidence of inappropriate loving, then praise be!

Can I love Peter Caddy appropriately? Yes, without any difficulty whatsoever. And when I think of him, I realise that there's a short cut that takes me straight to unconditional love. I remember his eyes: bright blue, shining with joy. They say that if you look into a person's eyes, you see their soul. The eyes contain the essence of the person. To remember Peter's eyes is to be with him, and more, it is to love him unconditionally. All his nonsense falls away. I don't have to accept it or even forgive it; it's simply not there anymore. But my last encounter with him was an unhappy one and I have to admit that the love I give is on the transpersonal level, on the spiritual plane if you will. On the personal level I still have reservations, which has been more my stuff than his, as I will tell later. With Eileen it is different. She radiates empathy and I love her unconditionally, both in her personality and in her soul.

*A Course in Miracles*, one of the many resources used at Findhorn, suggests that it is only in the other person that we see God. In Eileen's eyes I saw Wisdom and Compassion, in Peter's Joy in Action, and in both I saw God. I should add that Peter and Eileen both fit David Spangler's criteria of being powerful individuals with inclusive and interactive boundaries. I give them my unconditional love, which I now find has one special trait in common with 'falling in love'. It makes me feel supremely happy. I believe they feel that too.

*Exercise*

*Think of the person with whom you performed the previous exercise. Now remember their eyes and look deep into them. Stay looking for as long as you can, then release them with your blessing. Compare this experience of them with the previous one. Is there any difference? If so, start a journal and write it down. If not, don't worry, but still start a journal and write down your thoughts.*

Faith and Courage

I've been writing a lot about Peter Caddy and it's time I told you more about him. His life illustrates many of the qualities demanded of the unconditional lover. Peter loved God, and all his relationships were subject to that one ruling passion. His love was his faith. St. Paul calls faith "the evidence of things unseen," and Peter's faith was evident in his accomplishments. He made it the vehicle of manifestation, bringing ideas from the inner world into concrete reality despite all obstacles. A minister of the Unity Church once told him, "When you put your hand in the Lord's, hold onto your hat with the other hand." Peter's story tells how true this is.

Peter was trained in a secret Rosicrucian mystery school led by Dr. Sullivan, a surgeon who in World War Two worked for British Intelligence. From Dr. Sullivan he learned the precept, "To love where you are, to love who you are with, and to love the work you are doing." He developed an intuition which he learned to obey instantly and completely. These promptings would come to him in the midst of the most mundane affairs. "I was in Oban, Scotland, having breakfast," he once told us. "I needed to get to London, but had no transport and no money. Suddenly I had a prompting to go outside into the street, but I had just poured myself a cup of coffee, so I thought I would finish that first. When I got to the street, the expected ride had gone. It took me 24 hours and a lot of hassle to get to London."

Peter was a leader and a man of action who loved to cook. In World War Two he was a catering officer in the Royal Air Force and made his mark by introducing centralised messing to the sixty or so highly individualistic and competitive messes in a Bomber Wing. He was posted to India where he made use of every leave opportunity to lead climbing expeditions into the Himalayas. When the Group Captain, three ranks his senior and in command of ten thousand men, insisted on coming, Peter had concerns for the team's safety. He told him, "Well sir, you know you'll have to take orders from me, and just be one of the boys, having to peel potatoes and so on." The Group Captain took his turn peeling potatoes.

Peter was promoted to Squadron Leader and put in charge of all the RAF messes on the Burma front. Based in the sweltering heat of Calcutta, Peter put into practice Dr. Sullivan's precept, "to love the work you are doing," and had an extension cord fitted to his telephone so that he could conduct Command business from the swimming pool. Peter's success lay in his ability to inspire Dr. Sullivan's precepts in those under his command. Returning to Britain after the war, he married Sheena, a very spiritual woman, and was the first catering officer ever to be sent to the RAF Staff College, the elite school where officers are prepared for the highest echelons of the Force. Afterwards, he was posted to the Middle East where he travelled among the many RAF stations in the area.

Guided by his God-prompted intuition, Peter was even willing to put his career in jeopardy by pursuing a relationship with Eileen, the wife of a senior RAF colleague. Besides having a sense of humour, it seems that God doesn't always pay attention to the niceties of our social conventions. Eileen resisted Peter for some months but eventually fell deeply in love with him and asked her husband for a divorce. After enduring many hardships, Peter divorced Sheena and married Eileen. Later, he secured the position of manager of the three star Cluny Hill Hotel in Forres, Scotland.

Here, he once again put Dr. Sullivan's precepts into practice and, helped by Eileen's guidance, raised Cluny Hill Hotel to four star status. They now had three children and the future seemed bright. Peter was being his usual forthright self, commanding and demanding. He relished telling the story how he requisitioned several times for silver sauceboats for the dining room. Eventually his boss said the next van would bring them. "I unpacked the crate, and to my horror found that instead of silver, they had sent me the cheapest crockery. I knew the driver to be the boss' spy, so while he stood by astounded, I held out each one at arm's length and let it smash on the stone floor!"

But God still had a card to play. For no well defined reason, perhaps to rescue a struggling operation, perhaps for an earnest desire to see him fail, the company moved Peter to a hotel in perpetual difficulties: the Trossachs Hotel, in a beautiful location north of Glasgow. Here Peter's best efforts were defeated and he was fired. With no money and no job, but with a caravan that was very cramped for two adults and three children, Peter took his family north. Eileen felt assured that they would return to Cluny Hill, and he wished to be on the spot when the company directors changed their minds. They didn't, and the Findhorn Community was born.

On a snowy November day, he towed the caravan onto an old, sandy rubbish dump in the Findhorn Bay Caravan Park, the cheapest site available and the only one with space for a garden. Peter was never fazed by circumstance. The friends who had clustered round when he was manager of a four star hotel no longer looked at him when they met him in the street, for the rumour circulated that he had been fired for stealing; he signed on at the Labour Exchange for Unemployment Benefit and later for National Assistance, standing in line with many of his former employees; he applied for over two hundred jobs, but no one hired him. Eventually, a man from the National Assistance Board arrived with a thick file of Peter's failed efforts and, after questioning him closely, asked:

"Would you say that God is preventing you from getting a job?"

Amazed, Peter replied, "Yes, indeed."

"Well then, presumably if we cut off your money, God will also provide for you."

That's what they did, and that's what God did; for just at that time the first money from publishing Eileen's guidance began to come in.

This was not all. There were fairies at the bottom of Peter's garden. Dorothy Maclean, Peter's secretary from Cluny Hill, had come to join them and was receiving messages from the *devas*, the angelic presences that overlight plant species. Peter asked Dorothy to get their advice on gardening, and in a spirit of joyful co-operation, they began seeing what more could be done. The result was the famous 40 lb. cabbage, only one among a host of large and succulent vegetables. The Findhorn Garden became celebrated. For a long time Peter, unwilling to court weird publicity, insisted that it was only compost produced the results, but the gardening experts were not to be fooled. They looked at the sandy soil and shook their heads. At last, Peter confessed to the *devas*. Now the Community really took off, and the next few years saw immense growth that required all Peter's managerial resources of leadership, inspiration and patience. The Garden was now growing people rather than plants, and soon Peter found himself required to surrender his masculine qualities of dominance and discipline in favour of a gentler, more feminine approach. He found this hard, and began to withdraw, both from the Community and from Eileen, spending more time abroad, giving lectures and conducting workshops at which his charismatic showmanship excelled.

Peter devoted his life to God and expressed his devotion in service to the planet, grounding Light, wielding Truth and founding the Community that would continue to co-create with God. At the transpersonal level, throughout his life, he gave unconditional love to God and to the people involved in the Divine Plan with him. In his last years I am told he mellowed and began to love unconditionally at the personal level too. It was as if God had granted him grace and time to work on himself and clear up karma; he made pilgrimages to India and Brazil; he married twice more; and another son was born, with whom he made up for the time he hadn't spent with the others. His last wife, Renata, has a beautiful house overlooking Lake Constance in Germany. He settled there, and guess what? He set to work organising the garden! It was a shock to everyone when he died on the 18th of February 1994, killed near Lake Constance when his car collided with a van driving the wrong way across the highway.

Renata Caddy tells of the messages brought us by Peter's life. Among them: to have faith in God; to think big; to love what you do and see work as love in action; to have courage, be fearless and be happy. He envisioned the planet united in Light and Love and demonstrated that the universe rewards action. His qualities were many: discipline; obedience; intuition; charisma; leadership and love, but outstanding was his faith. His full story is told in his posthumous autobiography *In Perfect Timing*.

---

## 3. The Gap in the Ring

"The heart has its reasons that reason does not know."

*[Blaise Pascal]*

All right, you may say, you've known some really special people. How about the rest of us who haven't had such luck? Can we muster such faith? In whose eyes are we likely to see God manifest? Alas, that anyone should think it luck. We are all extraordinary and unique, special and individual aspects of God. That's why we're all different, and why one of Findhorn's watchwords is "Unity in Diversity."

But it's true, most people have difficulty with faith, and not many people's eyes are so transparent that you may see the Soul within. *A Course in Miracles'* actual words are, "May I behold you with the eyes of Christ and see my perfect sinlessness in you." That puts the responsibility on me, not the other person. It is I who must assume the eyes of Christ! How? At my usual ego-operating level, I may love others appropriately, but unconditional love is beyond me except in special cases. Compared to, say, Mother Teresa, my shortcomings are obvious. Can I rise to another level?

As I was addressing these issues, the image of a ring came to me, of the sort that so often appears in folklore. This was an iron ring that encompassed my heart, and its circle was not complete. There was a gap in the circle, the metal on either side terminating in a knob that I am sure was pierced so that a fastener could be drawn through to close it completely. If shut off, I would be lost. I recognised the two sides of the ring as the two sides of my egotistical nature, the one side that tends towards enthusiasm and excess and the other that tends towards lack and meanness. And sure enough, in the narrow gap between hovered a clear white light, signifying the Christ path. When I focused on that light, I realised that it is here that unconditional love becomes real. The effect is to raise my consciousness to a level above the ego. On the new level, what had appeared to the ego as opposites now appear as two parts of one whole. When I keep that illumined gap in my mind's eye, I operate at the level of the Christ path.

Some readers may find invocation of the Christ distasteful, smacking of a Christianity that in some of its branches has become elitist and punitive. But I have never believed in throwing the baby out with the bath water. At its most elementary, 'Christ' signifies to me an extraordinarily high level of consciousness, aware and self-actualising in all dimensions, and one that is the likely outcome of our evolutionary path. One can add deist implications if one wishes, but the bath water can stay down the drain for later recycling.

I am reminded of another part of my Findhorn experience, one that set me at odds with the community. My partner and I were drawing apart. I had come to the community with her and she was the mother of my son, but I was falling deeply in love with Kathy, a newcomer and a guest. My erstwhile partner was all in favour, seeing it as a way to release me gently, but the community could only see a predatory intruder who was breaking up an established family. Our Personnel Department, in charge of who stayed in the community and who left, consulted their spiritual guidance and took action to expel Kathy.

A word about spiritual guidance. Findhorn is founded on guidance. Eileen Caddy is clairaudient, meaning, in her case, that she actually hears God's voice when she 'goes within' in meditation. Over many years she has learnt to trust that voice. It is wise, practical, supportive, prescient and directed always to the highest good of all. Each morning in the early years of Findhorn, Eileen read out the guidance she had received for the community, and Peter ensured that whatever required action was done forthwith. Then came the day when Eileen announced that she had been told to no longer publish her guidance. Henceforth, each member should go within to find their own.

The community embarked on a very steep learning curve. The problem with guidance is that it is only as good as its source. Thoughts are real in the spiritual world and they can wander into your mind from all points of the compass: fragments of gossip from the nearby town; the thought form of the local parish church; your own egotistical desires. One's meditation must be deep, pure and centred if one is to contact one's true source, the Kingdom of God that Jesus said is within. This is why many people think it safer to abide by rules, but when conditions change, rules become roadblocks. Today's conditions have changed. The Age of Aquarius is here and Pisces is departing. Aquarian flexibility challenges Piscean rigidity. Today, a community or person who wants to be spiritually centred has really no alternative but to seek for their guidance (which will often tell them to abide by the rules), and to learn from their mistakes.

To return to the story. Personnel had told Kathy to leave. Coming back from the interview, she fell through some rotten planks in the steps up to her room and broke her ankle. Aghast that the community might be sued and perhaps admitting that their guidance had not been impeccable, Personnel rapidly changed track and came asking me what should be done. I told them that they should give my present partner other accommodation to her liking, that my injured Kathy would move in with me, and that we would both look after her.

For some time I held a grudge against the people in Personnel, at least one of whom I had counted as a friend, because they had not been open with us. Somehow they had got into their heads the false belief that we were engaged in a threesome, yet had never once addressed that issue openly. I remember talking with one of their number for an agonising 45 minutes, but that particular subject never came up. It was three months later, when I was 4,000 miles away, driving with Kathy in Texas, that my consciousness rose to the level of the Christ path – that gap in the ring – and I had a vision of that same member of Personnel sitting with me on a cloud, laughing over an open book that lay on our knees: perhaps the book with the story of our lives. Obviously the whole stupid train of events had a purpose within the divine plan: my relationship with Kathy was forged and tempered through stress and trial; we married and moved to the USA where we both work with the mentally and physically challenged; and our extended family has remained whole. It was at Findhorn that I learned that God makes use of our mistakes. But I haven't yet been able to bring that spiritual vision of unconditional love into my material existence. At my ego-operating level, I still think that the people in Personnel should have been honest with us!

It sounds hokey to say that we were sitting on a cloud, but that's how the etheric plane appears in visions. I believe it's the meaning behind the scripture that says we "shall see the Son of Man coming in the clouds with great power and glory." Spiritually, the world is divided into four planes or levels: Spirit, which is God consciousness; Soul or astral, which is the realm of the senses, emotions and intellect; Etheric, which holds life and memory; and the Material or mineral, which is the world we see with our physical eyes. Humans are incarnate on all four planes, though many are barely conscious of Spirit; animals are incarnate on the astral, etheric and mineral; plants on the etheric and mineral; and minerals just have the one. Where not incarnate, the other planes are present but excarnate: thus, Spirit and Soul are present in plants, but excarnate. As related to the human being, the etheric is a subtle body that permeates and extends a little beyond the physical and, with training, is perceptible to touch and vision.

Children tend to have this subtle sense. When I was focalising the Children's Programme at Findhorn, a Native American woman came to tell us how her people related to the natural world. The next day I had the idea of letting the children wander blindfolded in the local wood, to experience whether they could sense the etheric bodies of the trees before they bumped into them. For the first two minutes all went well. The children walked cautiously on the wood's edge but avoided the trees. Then, as they penetrated deeper, cries of distress rang out: "I can't find my way. There are trees all around me!" We hurried over to the child who was standing in an open space. Removing his blindfold, he looked amazed for that which was not there. Then I had an idea and scraped at the thick carpet of moss beneath our feet. Sure enough, we could see the stumps of trees, some old, some very old. Areas of the wood were felled every twenty years or so, but the memory of the trees, their etheric bodies, still stood.

When we look for our higher nature, I do not imagine that every one will have the same experience of an open ring as I did. Yet something like it must be a universal symbol for it perfectly illustrates the Bible's words, "strait is the gate and narrow is the way which leads to life." On either side lie the opposing evils, too little and too much. I imagine that the Christ path may appear as a bright light, a secret part of the self, a deep intuition. However it appears, I believe it will be recognisable, and if so, trustworthy. The more we live in it, the stronger and more informative it becomes.

Forgiveness is married to unconditional love. Real forgiveness must be distinguished from dismissiveness, the feeling that the offence, whatever it was, is not big enough to justify a lasting grudge with all the attendant inconveniences. If we love unconditionally, forgiveness becomes an instinct, as Jesus demonstrated when the soldiers nailed him to the cross: "Father, forgive them for they know not what they do." Unconditional love comes from the heart consciousness, but because most of us live primarily in our heads, it helps, when we suffer injury, to recognise our anger and resentment as signals and direct our thoughts instead to the Christ path.

Of course, our ego operating level will not let up. It will speak out, demanding recompense or revenge. The lack side of our ego will persist for as long as we have a physical body, but it helps to recognise its voice and wait for the Higher Self, which knows the Christ path, to respond. And when we feel resentment, to look beyond dismissiveness. Unfortunately, as demonstrated in my bout with Personnel, the higher purposes inherent in events often do not become plain until later. Patience, it seems, is part of God's Lesson Plan.

Unconditional love and real forgiveness are both transformative. No one can resist what is offered. Both giver and receiver are forever changed. But I think that many people get discouraged when they find that there's no permanence to the high that is experienced. Soon they return to 'normal' consciousness, perhaps to its depths. I think this is a necessary part of the human experience. It's called 'grounding'.

During my first year at Findhorn I went through a grounding experience when Peter Caddy asked me to focalise the Children's Programme. Initially, this was only to be a child-minding respite for the parents who were attending the Education Department's courses, but our cohorts immediately devised a plan for a real children's education programme. The first week it went swimmingly; everything was perfect. However, in the following weeks we had to struggle to hold it together. It was as if we had been shown the vision of perfection at the start of the process, and then had to ground it in all our personality facets as the project proceeded.

*Exercise*

*Have you ever had the sense of being 'guided'; as if someone or something was reaching in to do you a good turn or prevent an accident? Was that just luck or an angel leaving a calling card? Doesn't matter. Nothing happens by chance. Focus on that event or moment in time and let yourself be filled with gratitude. Carry that feeling through your day. Make time to write down in your journal any insights that come to you.*

---

## 4. AN ENCOUNTER

"Always remember that all roads lead to Me."

*[Eileen Caddy]*

Can role models help us focus on unconditional love and maintain us in that loving state? I think the answer is yes, but only in certain circumstances. A personal interaction is needed, one that involves all the senses. You must be ready for it and unafraid, for it feels as if every cell in your body comes alive and shouts for joy. It may be only a timeless moment that is involved, but it partakes of the nature of eternity: over in an instant, remaining with us forever. At the age of ten a friend of mine met the Mahatma Gandhi in person and decided that henceforth she would look for the best in human nature and devote her life to its portrayal. Soon afterwards, she was given her own children's programme on Radio India and has since been involved in some very successful movies and TV series. There are many role models on planet earth and very few of them are famous like the Mahatma or Mother Teresa: we may encounter them in old people's homes, among the physically and mentally challenged, and among ordinary people, often in humble walks of life. And the spiritual world is always ready to lend a hand, waiting for the right circumstances to occur.

I once experienced this in rather dramatic fashion when I asked a simple question. I was living at Findhorn and feeling down and disenchanted. Though I did not realise it, the time for my departure was drawing near. I asked myself, "Why am I here?" Suddenly, it was as if a silent movie was unrolling inside my head. I knew myself in a Viking incarnation about a thousand years earlier. Raiding along the coasts and rivers of Britain, Ireland and France, I had been one of the worst of men, brave and ruthless, feared even among my own kind for I was prone to settle arguments with a knife thrust. What faith I had was given to Thor and Odin, and I had some hopes of Valhalla where the souls of heroes gather to feast and fight while awaiting the Day of the Last Battle. My chief hatred was reserved for the adherents of the 'White Christ', as we Norsemen called the Christian God. His teachings of love and forgiveness were especially offensive to my way of life. My predecessors had robbed his monasteries of nearly all their valuables, but the monks and nuns were still there, praying. The older ones I killed, but the younger ones made good slaves and I sold them in the wealthy markets of Moorish Spain. They would not be asked to break their vows of poverty and obedience, but they would have to forego chastity. I was justification for the old English prayer, "From the fury of the Norsemen, good Lord preserve us!"

These practices enriched me and I attracted a band of ferocious followers. However, a large part of my success derived from a life I spared. I had captured the abbess of one of the more important convents. She was not young or comely enough to fetch much in the market, and I debated whether to kill her. She saw my thought, for she was very intelligent, and urged me to keep her with me, telling me that she knew where monasteries had hidden their remaining gold and silver, and that she could influence the captive nuns to cease their wailing and accept their lot. This would be useful, for some were so desperate that they starved themselves and arrived in Spain thin, bedraggled and nearly worthless. More for her courage than her inducements, for she had not panicked when she divined my murderous intent, I saved her life. For many years that proved well for me, for the advice she gave was as good as she had promised. I even left her in charge of my ship when raiding inland, and eventually I took her as my wife.

Time came when my limbs grew stiff and I realised, reluctantly, that my Viking days were over. My reputation had made me unwelcome in many of the Norse communities to which I might have retired, but the Earl of Orkney needed just such a one as I to keep his stronghold of Burghead, an isolated enclave on the north-east coast of Scotland. It was on a rocky peninsula, easily defensible, and I took service with him, taking charge of the township, establishing my wife as chatelaine in the great hall, starting a sea wall to protect the harbour, which was exposed to gales, and repairing the timber palisade on the defensive earthwork on the landward side. I hoped to make it a base for younger warriors to raid and settle along the coast and set up a Norse hegemony to counter the growing power of the Christian Pictish Kingdom centred on Inverness, a bare forty miles to the west. This ambition proved my undoing.

Little trade came to the isolated town and we depended for subsistence on fish brought in by our small fleet of in-shore boats and on the produce of the good farmland that lay round about the town. I was keen to extend my boundaries into the waste of gorse and heather that lay between my farms and Pictland, clearing the ground as I did so. Thinking to provoke me, the Pictish

King contrived an incident. Five of my men were surprised and killed. I resolved to punish him by burning his castle at Forres, about five hours' march distant. My wife's rather stolid face grew heavy when I told her my plans. Three days were spent repairing armour, sharpening weapons and gathering provisions. Ordinarily, so much time would not be needed, but my wife insisted that the Picts would retaliate and we should prepare to withstand a siege. On the third night, early, I led out all my able-bodied men, some ninety of them, leaving my wife to guard the walls with women and men too old or sick to march. I planned to attack the castle at dawn, spend the next two days ravaging the countryside and return to Burghead on the third, driving my captured cattle and prisoners before me. It would be like the old days, but with a dry and comfortable bed at the end of it, not the damp timbers of shipboard.

My approach to Forres lay between the marshes of Findhorn Bay on my right and the length of Cluny Hill huddling close above on my left. The castle stood under the further end of the hill, beside a small stream that emptied into the bay. I could see my men straggling in a long file behind me as I came below the hill. I would delay massing them in battle-ready formation, because that was a noisy, jostling business in the dark and would alert the enemy. I counted on the element of surprise.

The hill was crowned with beech trees that extended some way down its slope. I had just come opposite its midpoint when the night air was filled with Pictish war cries and I saw their small ponies emerge from the trees. Taken in the flank, my hopelessly vulnerable line would melt under the Pictish onslaught, and for the first and last time my berserk courage left me as I realised my wife had betrayed me. Finding herself so close to their lands again, she had had an access of Christian conscience, thinking that her pagan husband's death would ensure her own salvation. I turned to flee, shouting to all who could to save themselves, and to burn my wife if they got back to Burghead. I do not think any did.

Refusing to be cut down from behind, I made a stand in front of a low bank that lay across my path. A thorn tree grew above it, giving some scant protection to my back. The three horsemen following me dismounted and approached warily. The death thrust was swift and deep, and they stood back to watch me die. As the lifeblood ebbed onto the marshy ground, I saw a mist form in front of me. My eyes watched it coalesce and take shape, and I felt the shock of utter horror as I recognised the White Christ. Here was my worst enemy come to gloat as I lay powerless, about to die. I had heard of the Christian Hell and expected no better.

Then he spoke. "You have deserved Valhalla. Will you go there?"

I looked into his eyes and saw my dearest friend. "No, Lord," I said, "I will follow you."

Rudolf Steiner says that those who have once experienced the Christ have no difficulty believing in him through all their subsequent incarnations. So it has been for me. I rather suspect that, in those lives immediately following, my enthusiasm went overboard and I served the Inquisition; too new to the whole concept to have learned discrimination, my soul was irresistibly drawn to whatever claimed to serve Jesus. It was another case of having the perfect experience and then having to work through it and ground it in each part of the personality.

There is a scriptural passage which speaks of the stone which the builders rejected, which has become the cornerstone, most important in the building: "Whosoever shall fall upon that stone shall be broken, but on whomsoever it shall fall, it will grind him to powder." This saying refers to the consequences of the Christ experience. All the traits and facets of personality painstakingly built up over previous lives must be taken apart and put together again on a new model. The image is of a clay pot smashed into a thousand pieces. I had built up quite a satisfactory personality, given the time and conditions, and now it was utterly useless. You may ask, then what is the benefit of the Christ experience? From this point in my evolution I can answer that it is the knowledge, deep within myself, of a very powerful and loving friend who takes extraordinary pains to show me the right path and guard my safety: he is The Beloved in whom all my other beloveds are subsumed.

Over the succeeding lives, quite a few I think, I have been building a new personality, working through my karma. Some new traits are emerging, some old traits have been modified. I am not as brave as I once was – only by necessity now, as the hobbit said – and I am more thoughtful. Karma demands that we are accountable for our actions: we want to experience the consequences of all our good deeds and make restitution for all our bad ones. I have had enough bad karma for several lifetimes and more than once, up against a brick wall, I suspect I have contemplated suicide. I hope I had enough sense to say no. Suicide doesn't let you escape from life. You are immortal, and you merely acquire more bad karma. It seems that it is irresponsible to reject life's offerings, even when they are horrible. I suppose this is why the Roman Catholic Church rejects euthanasia, even for the terminally ill and suffering, heartless though that seems.

In some deep core of my being those eyes still hold me. The unconditional love they gave me, despite who I was, is a love I must return, not only to the Giver but through him to all humankind and all the denizens of the planet, seen and unseen. Each life is spent learning how to do so. I must do what I most desire. To my mind, that is how karma works, not as a fate inflicted on you for deeds good or bad, but as something you freely choose, because in no other way can you evolve spiritually and be happy. As you come closer to the fount of Being, progress is Joy. Unconditional love does not bind, it frees.

*Exercise*

*Was there a time in your life when you were at a cross-roads, not knowing which way to turn? Perhaps despairing, no options left? Or just feeling that you were stuck in a dead end career, or one you didn't particularly enjoy? What got you out of there? Think of the turning point, whatever it was, an opening, an inspiration, a friend's suggestion, or simply your own decision. Settle yourself comfortably to meditate on that moment and, if it will, let it speak to you.*

*If you are lucky enough to have escaped getting stuck or despairing, do the same with any moment that made you feel happy or grateful.*

*Or, if you still feel stuck or despairing, let yourself experience the feeling, commit yourself to the Highest and ask to be shown a way out.*

*Write down your insights in your journal.*

---

## 5. Why?

"There are more things in heaven and earth,
Horatio, than are dreamt of in your philosophy."
*[William Shakespeare]*

I think most readers will think I have some explaining to do. First, do I really feel that this 'movie flash', of which the essentials lasted about 45 seconds, was the true experience of a prior lifetime? I have to admit that I don't know. It felt real enough. The emotions were in place along with the pictures, but as if coming from a great distance. Such experiences are called 'far memory'. It had a purpose, teaching me that unconditional love arises in the spiritual world and is truly inclusive. Many spiritual experiences come as a surprise and this was no exception. The whole thing was unexpected, always a good test of truthfulness. And I don't think any element of wish-fulfilment was involved, for I had never sought for past-life experiences, believing that I had quite enough to deal with in my present life. Rather my prayer had been that I should not experience them until they were relevant to me. Suddenly, they were!

The more important question is why the God of Christianity should appear and offer me a choice – Odin's heaven or his own – after I had spent a lifetime trying to destroy his work. Hell was not even mentioned. If we can answer this question, it won't matter whether the experience was 'real' or not, because it will have been virtually real. I think the answer lies in one word, intensity. As a Norseman, my hatred of the Christ had consumed me. All my focus was on him. Inevitably, we invoke that on which we focus. We think of a person, and at some level that person is aware. People will quite often remark on such 'coincidences'; they think of someone they have not seen for a while and find a postcard from them waiting in their mailbox. Had I been an ordinary pirate, looting for gold and silver, I do not believe the experience would have happened. The intensity of my hatred for Christ and his teaching, my commitment to destroy his Church, those were the drives that brought him to me. I invoked him. Of course, he waited till I was vulnerable – he's not stupid – and it was a simple choice he offered – his way or mine. Though, thinking about it, it wasn't really a choice. I knew him for the other part of me. There's no way I could have refused him.

This story challenges many people's version of God – the Judge of Sinners. They will ask why he did not condemn me. He might have forgiven the soldiers who nailed him to the cross, but surely his faithful servants whom I had slaughtered deserved something more from him? My deeds called for punishment. I deserved Hell. Was he just playing with me, giving me a chance to repent, to condemn me later if my grades weren't good enough? Those eyes tell me different. They were innocent of guile and calculation. They live in the ever present Now, and Now I am his friend.

These five assertions – our immortality, reincarnation, lives as learning, the absence of judgement and the absoluteness of unconditional love – are at such variance with traditional Christian teaching that some of my readers may be finding them hard to swallow. They deserve more examination and, as I promised at the beginning of the first chapter, they will get it. In fact, they hang together, and any one without the others does not make sense. To put the boot on the other foot, I would suggest that it is the traditional teachings of Christianity that do not make sense. As a boy I had the hardest time with them. I was a privileged child, attending private boarding schools where morning prayers on weekdays and church on Sundays were compulsory. I was that bugbear of teachers, a child with a critical mind, and so much exposure to church led me to ask some precocious questions: how did the crucifixion assure the salvation of humankind? How did the process work? What were its mechanics? Or failing those, its logic? I was told, "You must have faith" or "Some things are beyond human understanding." I found totally insufficient the suggestion that Jesus was simply an example, to show the way. I felt deep sympathy for the schoolboy who, asked to define faith, wrote that it was believing what you know to be untrue.

That might have been the end of it for me, except that I knew, deep within me, that there was a core of truth somewhere and that it related to Jesus, who seemed inexplicably real to me. I began to find the answers in Rudolf Steiner's lectures and writings. Steiner was a philosopher and mystic who was active at the end of the nineteenth century and the beginning of the twentieth. Born in Croatia, then a part of the Austro-Hungarian Empire, he based himself in Germany but travelled extensively to give lectures in Western Europe. He began the Waldorf system of education, which now has schools in many countries (the Moray Steiner School is associated with Findhorn); he initiated biodynamic farming; founded the Anthroposophical Society; and created much else. His lectures and writings are still in print and extend to over two hundred volumes, but it was his teachings on the Being of Christ Jesus that chiefly attracted me. Steiner sees humanity's goal as the spiritualisation of matter, a teaching which is reflected in the Church's doctrine of the Resurrection of the Body.

I should emphasise that Steiner's is not the official doctrine at Findhorn, for there is none. It's just one of the many threads – Sai Baba, Alice Bailey, Transcendental Meditation, Gurdjieff, *A Course in Miracles*, Christianity, Eileen and Peter Caddy – that make up the tapestry of lore and teaching there. However, Steiner's universe is one where unconditional love is not only possible but necessary. It provides an alternative mental framework for anyone brought up in a society moulded by the traditional Christian paradigm. The traditional model is self-contradictory and puts unnecessary obstacles in the path of mental understanding. Let me elaborate. I was taught as a child that if I put temptation in someone's way and they fell victim to it, I was as guilty as they. How does that work for the God of the Garden of Eden? Further, the Bible maintains that He is a loving God, who yet condemns those of his 'children' who disobey his rather whimsical commands to an eternal Hell. Over nearly two millennia, our efforts to justify these contradictions has led to a schizoid culture in the West, particularly in the USA where Judaic-Christian beliefs dominate.

There are individual Christians, in the Church and outside it, who rise above these contradictions and are magnificent examples of unconditional love. St. Francis of Assisi, Mother Teresa, Pope John XXIII and Dr. Rowan Williams, Archbishop of Canterbury, spring to mind. However, observing their lives and philosophies, I think they come from the heart rather than the head. And since we in the West have been primarily educated to use our heads, I believe it will help us personally to love unconditionally if we have Steiner's model of divine love before us, just as an alternative.

When I was very young I was told that there was a Recording Angel in Heaven who wrote down all my doings in a book. I gathered that he was more interested in my misdeeds than my few good behaviours, which were probably not worth consideration because expected of me. I do not think the tale improved my conduct much but it probably implanted the beginnings of a guilty conscience. But what if a legend, which folk misused to restrain their children's naughtiness, has yet some truth behind it? The etheric body holds memory, and Earth has an etheric body. People can train themselves to read that memory. They call it the Akashic Record. All events of spiritual significance throughout earth's entire history are remembered there. Those accessing that memory experience the events like an observer, seeing and hearing them as they occurred. Steiner was adept at reading the Akashic Record and his teachings about Jesus were based on his direct vision of the action as it actually happened.

I can accept that the Akashic Record exists because I once found myself reading it. I was on the island of Skye, which clearances and neglect have largely reduced to wasteland. I found myself tapping into the memory of the landscape, where it was dreaming of the time when human beings had worked it and cared for it. The fields, the cattle, the red-kirtled women, even the small fortress and reed-thatched hall that had housed the young men, I could see all of them with an inner eye; but with the outer eye, just a few banks that were reminders of the fields, and on a hilltop a pile of stones that looked unnatural. I have a sceptical mind, despite what you may think, and I naturally questioned the veracity of my observations. Later in the day I came upon a road beside a sea loch, where across the water I could see trees waving joyously, for a gale was blowing. Except that there were no trees there. The hill was as bald as a shaven head. A few yards away an elderly man was filling a pothole in the road.

"Have there ever been trees on that hill?" I asked.

He stared at it for about half a minute and I wondered if he saw what I did. Then he replied slowly, "There must have been. In the Gaelic, the name (of the hill) is Forest."

I can accept the reality of the Akashic Record. Whether Steiner's reading of the Record as relates to Jesus is correct, you must be the judge. He has said himself that everyone's interpretation of the Record is filtered through the personality and, in that way, biases do creep in. So please consult your own truth.

The story begins with Time itself. In the original Hebrew, the word used in the first chapter of Genesis for the Creator God is 'Elohim', which is actually a plural form. After the creation story the word used is 'El', singular. The first chapter is not a record of a physical creation: plants were created before the sun. It tells of creation on the astral or soul level. Chapter Five recounts the generations of Adam and verse two is emphatic, "Male and female created he them; and blessed them, and called their name Adam." On the astral plane humanity was one soul with both male and female characteristics. In the second chapter creation descends to the etheric level, and the story switches to Eden and the incarnating plant kingdom. Sexual division is occurring and Eve appears beside Adam. Etheric sex is innocent and they are unaware of their nakedness. Adam and Eve made the descent to the physical plane in defiance of the divine order, which had assigned humanity to a plane no lower than the etheric. That was the Fall. The Elohim allowed the Fall to occur although they were the guardians of Humanity. Never mind that we engineered the Fall of our own free will – after all, Humanity is the Son of God and we used the Father's power. If you are a Creator, you are responsible for what you create.

It was not wilfulness that led to our decision to incarnate. A physical incarnation offers tremendous opportunities that are otherwise unavailable to pure Spirit. There were risks of course along with the opportunities. Legend says that it was Lucifer, not Satan, who tempted us. Lucifer means 'Lightbearer', and it is my fantasy that he was fed up with the way matter blocked his passage and persuaded us to undertake its spiritualization, to give out its own light. Satan is actually a human creation. The name comes from an ancient Sanskrit word that still survives in several languages, as words with crude meanings tend to. It refers to human excrement, and the derivation is plainer in his Arabic name, 'Sheitan'. His existence derives from the fact that, just as all physical objects have an etheric form, so they must have a soul and spirit form also. These are the 'Ideas' of Plato's philosophy, the living Principles that underlie all earthly creation. "*Alles Irdiches ist nur ein Gleichniss*, All earthly things are but a likeness," wrote Goethe. It holds true for the highest and the most base.

Our physical bodies have to dispose of waste. Satan represents everything that is no longer useful to humankind: stuff from which we have extracted the benefit and whose continued presence in us is destructive. Having come into existence through our defiance of God's will, Satan is opposed to God in everything. If God's will is Abundance, then Lack and Famine are Satan's instruments. Stone is one of his symbols: good in itself, but when taken into the human being, it becomes the stonyhearted man. When Jesus renamed his apostle Simon, calling him Peter, meaning 'stone', and making him the foundation of his Church, he issued Satan with the ultimate challenge: that he would leave him no piece of earth on which to stand. In a sense, Peter is Satan's representative among the apostles. He was given the Keys of the Kingdom, to lock the Gates behind him after the rest of humanity has entered.

Satan will be with us as long as we have a physical body, but he was not present before the Fall. Lucifer stands in a different category. He is one of the original principles of the divine creation, the Lightbearer, overleaping bounds: in the human being, Excess. Too much and two little are the two principles of evil. The representatives of both were present when the Son of Man was crucified. Remember the two robbers on either side of him? One blessed, the other cursed him: Lucifer and Satan respectively.

By allowing the Fall to occur, the Elohim had incurred a karmic debt. Yes, karma works for the Gods too! How else would we have accountability and responsibility in our multi-dimensional creation? Their challenge now was to return us, with all the gifts acquired through our many lives on the material plane, to the purity and innocence of Spirit – to the Kingdom of God. The Elohim chose to do this by becoming human, to experience every facet of what humanity now was.

Certain devices were necessary. The Jews' strict dietary and marriage laws prepared a suitable physical body in descent from Abraham. A soul body was prepared over an even longer period. The generational records given in Matthew and Luke summarise the process, which can be further explored in Steiner's lectures on the respective Gospels. An infant's, even a child's body could not contain the resplendent consciousness of the Godhead, so it was at the baptism in Jordan that the Elohim descended to the human Jesus and began their karmic task: to ensure that all humanity should return to the consciousness of God's Kingdom. Nothing less would wipe out the debt. This concept of the all-inclusiveness of the Return – salvation and redemption are the terms used by the Church – is confirmed in the Archangel Michael's communications with Ana Pogacnik, as related by her father Marko in his book *Christ Power and the Earth Goddess*. Michael (he prefers to be so addressed. 'Saint' makes for too much distance) is concerned that we people are unready for the forthcoming earth changes, which will radically alter physical nature, but he reiterates, "No one will be left behind."

The Elohim had chosen to become human, but there was still a problem. To be fully human, a person must experience death, and a God cannot die. The Church encountered this difficulty when they first tried to win converts in India: Hindus, who had long experience of divinity, objected that, for a divine being, crucifixion was not merely disgusting and inappropriate, but impossible. The Elohim could not die – on several occasions during Jesus' ministry, an angry populace tried to lay hands on him, only to find that they could not. However, over the three years of the Elohim's passage on earth, a human personality, wholly pure, loving and innocent, was growing up under their tutelage. This is the being known as the Son of Man, to whom Jesus increasingly referred during his lifetime. It is usually thought that he was referring to himself, but in fact it was to an aspect of himself. After Gethsemane, the Elohim withdrew, and it was the Son of Man who was taken to be tried, crowned with thorns, flogged and crucified.

The Son of Man is crucial to our evolution. Steiner tells us that he is so simple that he can relate to every human being. He can love us unconditionally, and through that love we are transformed and able to pass it on to others. When we love unconditionally, we are present in the Kingdom, whatever our material situation: witness Mother Teresa. For me, these insights provide the answers to my boyhood questions about the logic and mechanics of the Christian story of redemption. The logic is karmic necessity, the mechanics is the immanence of the Son of Man: his continued presence in the body of Earth and his ability to inspire unconditional love in every human being, however base.

I believe it was the Son of Man whom I met beside that marshy bay so long ago. It's not been easy. I'm still working through the karma of that Viking incarnation, helping those I harmed, working with those who helped me. There's a lot to do and undo. To try to avoid our karma would be to resign from life completely. Every last tiny action shall be accounted for. Even that unsatisfactory interaction with Findhorn's Personnel Department was payback of a sort. I had a vision later of the man with whom I had that tiresome conversation. He had been a bishop in my Viking days, and had worn a handsome gold cross set with amethysts that I coveted. Far memory or wishful thinking? Either way, I should forgive him for not asking me outright whether we were engaged in a threesome. After all, my Viking self had never asked for his permission to kill him. I can't forgive myself for that deed, and know I have more work to do with him.

Far memory is not for the squeamish, and it's a good thing that most of us can do without it. I need to forgive others, but forgiving myself is a luxury I can afford when I've worked through my karma. Unconditional love does not require you to forgive yourself, just to forgive the other person and give them the love.

*Exercise*

*Take a moment to consider the alternative view of God and humankind presented in this chapter. Does it offer a framework for you to make choices that are discriminating but non-judgemental, help practice your intuition and seize opportunities? If so, consider how you should proceed. Write down your thoughts.*

*Or are you disturbed and upset that so many cherished beliefs should be challenged? Or indifferent? Then go beyond your beliefs now, feel the love at the core of your being, ready waiting behind your Soul, love that is beyond all logic and all questions. Bathe in it, rest in it, linger there, know it is with you always. Write down your insights.*

---

# 6. The Perennial Philosophy

"You are the point of light within My mind.
You are the point of love within My heart."

*[Eileen Caddy]*

Several meanings have been suggested for the word 'religion'. I prefer Robert Graves', who derives it from the Latin *re-ligare*, 'to bind back'. This would indicate that there was a time when humans lived in closer communion with their gods, or with nature, and that the rituals of religion were designed to bring the consciousness of that state back into the minds of the congregation. This makes anthropological and linguistic sense. As related by Laurens van der Post, the Bushmen of the Kalahari lived in communion with nature. The hunter would know when he woke in the morning where to find the eland that he was to kill that day, so that his family might survive. The eland would know too and be in accord. The Pope's title, *Pontifex Maximus* 'the greatest bridge builder', is descended from the High Priests of ancient Rome and signifies that he is to bridge the gap that has opened between the material and spiritual worlds.

Observers have remarked that those who have advanced furthest in their religion, though of different faiths, have broadly the same experiences. We usually call them mystics. In ancient Greece, such was Diogenes and, later, the neo-Platonist Plotinus, also the practitioners of the Jewish Kabala, Islamic Sufis, Cathars and Rosicrucians, St. John of the Cross, and in modern times, Teilhard de Chardin, Tagore and William James, to mention only a very few. The similarity of mystical experience has led to the proposition that there is a perennial philosophy that is the foundation of all religions and unites them. Theologies are as different as the races and times that bore them, but experience at the deep, inner core of spiritual activity is similar. Some ideas, the more pacific ones, are also similar, for example that the Good, the True and the Beautiful are expressions of the Divine and that what is good for the one is good for the whole.

Religions are like pearls on three interlocking chains, Sun, Moon and Earth inspired, and make a complete circle reflecting humankind. Each religion is appropriate to the particular people at the particular time that it appears. It speaks to the particular consciousness of God that has evolved in that place and carries it forward. Thus, a religion relates primarily to the level of enlightenment amongst its adherents, and only secondarily to the nature of their God. However, if a good man prays to his God, of whatever religion, it should be obvious that the same good God will answer him. Therefore we can say that the Christ is to be found in every religion, meaning as I suggested earlier, that it will contain the path to an extraordinarily high level of consciousness, aware and self-actualising in a universe of dimensions: God consciousness in fact.

In the twentieth century various sorts of scientific agnosticism have become dominant, spurred by the development of intellect, which has effectively killed off the clairvoyant vision which was the underpinning of the age of faith. We believe what we perceive, and most of us no longer perceive the spiritual realms. This is not a disaster, but a necessary step in our evolution towards freedom. We cannot be truly free if we are aware at every instant of heaven looking over our shoulder, telling us what to do. When we have only our own moral sense to distinguish right from wrong, then we are truly free and in the course of repeated lives learn to know who we are: part of the Godhead. There is then no conflict between duty and freedom, for when we reach that level, we are so subsumed with love for the Whole that what we most want to do is what we have to do. I think of the cells in a healthy body, each conscious of itself both as an individual and as a functioning part of the whole. I do not think of atheists and agnostics as divorced from God, but as being very close, for they have courageously followed their truth. It is significant that it was an agnostic medical researcher, totally devoted to objective fact, who channelled *A Course in Miracles*. Of course, she was dismayed at what she was doing and consented to publication only after prolonged exhortations by her friends. Who says that God doesn't have a sense of humour?

Instead of being competitive, we may view the world's religions, and science too, as co-operative, working sometimes together and sometimes in opposition to bring humanity closer to God. This is the reverse of the usual view propagated by some scientists and the many varieties of priests and faithful, who want their path to be the only one. Indeed, Steiner tells us that the central figures of three major religions, the Lord Krishna, Gautama Buddha and Zarathustra, attended and co-operated in the birth and youth of Jesus. The intense spirituality of Islam appeared later. On the physical plane these religions are often opposed, for it is the nature of the human being to demand absolutism and uniformity of belief. So we have religions that are isolative and combative, spreading their version of the Word to other peoples, especially conquered ones, without regard to the truth and cultural value of the religions they are trying to supplant. Yet such opposition may sometimes force the consciousness forward, making us redefine our beliefs and values in a way that maintenance of a complacent *status quo* will never accomplish. We will have more to say on this subject in Chapter 16 when we discuss the role of evil, but next let us discuss the concept of reincarnation, which so many people in the West find doubtful or repugnant.

The ideas of reincarnation and karma weave themselves into the perennial philosophy as the moral glue which holds creation together. Balance is vital, but is opposed by the need to explore, develop, evolve, in a word, *live!* So whoever takes a new initiative is responsible for its outcome, to see that balance is restored. Every action we take, every word we say, is just such an initiative. So reincarnation and karma are the means, mechanism if you will, by which balance is maintained and restored. Christians have particular difficulty with these ideas. Brought up to believe in a loving God who will send them to Hell if they are disobedient, and taught that our existence here is 'a vale of tears', the prospect of repeated lives is frightening. They have despaired of the dichotomy and opted for a safe heaven to which they will go after a single life. Far better to have an omnipotent God who takes care of everything and will provide a mansion for those who have lived moderately blamelessly, there to experience the ideal of an upper class existence. I think it was Simone du Beauvoir in her book *The Second Sex* who remarked on the disastrous effect of the 4th Century Church fathers on Christian thinking. Ecstatic to be part of the establishment at last, they modelled their idea of heaven on the rituals of the imperial Byzantine court.

The Emperor Constantine 's conversion to Christianity led naturally to the idea that the Church must uphold the state; if it didn't, it would be persecuted again. People living godly and upright lives have a large investment in the *status quo* and make for obedient subjects. So the idea caught on. Consequently the idea of reincarnation is anathema in the Church. "You can't let people think they have a second chance," is how one good friend, an Anglican priest, put it to me. Never mind the truth. At least he was honest. Actually, both Old and New Testaments contain indications that reincarnation was an accepted possibility. For example, the Hebrew word sometimes translated as 'generations' is derived from a Sanskrit root which means 'turning of a wheel'. In Buddhism, the same word is used for the 'Wheel of Life', i.e., the cycle of repeated incarnations. And Jesus' question, "Whom do men say that I am?" and the answer, "Some say John the Baptist, some say Elia; and others Jeremias" (Mat.16:13–14) indicates a local acceptance of the idea of reincarnation.

In esoteric literature, the accounts of Jesus' and earlier times affirm that all contemporary religions, Jewish included, conducted initiation rituals for their brighter priests; the primary lesson learned was the experience of reincarnation. Within the inner recesses of the temple, the candidate was placed in a coffin where he 'died' and passed into the underworld; after three days, he was ritually brought to life again by the High Priest. Steiner relates that the raising of Lazarus, conducted outside the temple and in public, violating the innermost secrets of their religion, was the act that motivated the priests of the Sanhedrin to put Jesus to death.

I have already mentioned Plato's thesis that all material objects are manifestations of ideas in the spiritual world. Principles like beauty and intellect are also manifestations of spiritual 'ideas'. Polytheism was based on the ancient ability to perceive these principles on their non-physical, i.e., etheric or astral planes; animism likewise used the same ability in respect of physical objects. Expert practitioners could manipulate these manifestations for the benefit of their society and became leaders, with names like priest, magician or witch doctor. The account of their practices, told in Sir James Frazer's *The Golden Bough* is accurate, but not his conclusion, that their beliefs had no substance.

Earth itself has an inhabiting spirit called by various names, e.g., *Gaia* both today and in ancient Greece, and *Sophia* in the lands where the Eastern Orthodox Church is paramount. This is a female entity and I believe that it is now joined and united with a masculine one, none other than the Son of Man. Consider what we are told. The gospels relate that when the spear pierced Jesus' side, blood and water flowed unmingled to the ground. Blood is the vehicle of a person's spiritual essence, so it was Jesus' spiritual essence that was entering Earth. The event was accompanied by an earthquake, when the veil of the Temple in Jerusalem was torn in two. That veil separated the public from the sacred parts of the Temple, and its tearing signified that henceforth the public and the sacred should be one. It is said that in Ireland, where the old clairvoyant vision was preserved, seers saw the aura of the Earth change.

If we accept the truth of these accounts and follow their logic, it means that Christ, the ultimate consciousness, has not left the earth. In the being known as the Son of Man, he has remained with us as he promised. All earth, and all that lives and rests upon it, visible and invisible, is transformed by his presence. The sacraments of bread and wine are not mere symbols, but real, containing the presence bestowed by the Creator God. Sri Krishna, Lakshmi, Tara, Quan Yin, Sophia, the Blessed Virgin Mary and the Son of Man may each manifest to a believer and offer that same irresistible and unconditional love that I encountered. I am very far from being alone. Mystics in all religions have given their own descriptions of the divine presence. Marko Pogacnik describes his experiences of Sophia's sweet female energy in *Daughter of Gaia*, and his perception of Christ's presence at the Catholic Mass in *Christ Power and the Earth Goddess*.

Unconditional love transforms, and I see this as the destiny of humankind. There is no avoiding it, however much we may try to excuse ourselves. With every bite of food we eat, with every drink we take, with each breath of air, we partake of the Godhead. We do not need the Church's blessing to make it a sacrament, though it helps to live mindfully and avoid artificial foods that are not grown naturally, especially meats from animals that have been mistreated. Poultry and pigs reared in factory farms, calves reared for the white tenderness of their veal, and geese force-fed to fatally enlarge their livers for paté de foie gras, all accumulate karma for those who raise them and those who eat them. We are what we eat. We will pay our karmic dues, even the gods cannot avoid that, but nonetheless we are promised the grace of unconditional love. We will all re-enter the Kingdom of God, because nothing less will satisfy the karmic debt incurred by our Creator and Guardian Godhead.

We need to ground this discussion of lofty principles with the example of one who, to her vast surprise, received the unconditional love of God when she was enmeshed in a passionate and adulterous relationship, lost to her family and society. She learned to return that love with steadfast constancy, and in the end found all her dreams fulfilled. Of the many qualities that go into the love she shows, the one that stands out in my mind is her capacity to endure; and yet the touchstone that changed her life, at its most abysmal moment, was gratitude.

Endurance

I think that all Eileen Caddy wanted of life was a good marriage and a lot of children and grandchildren. She got the children, and Peter and God's unconditional love too, and went through a lot of trouble for all of them. Brought up in the waning days of Britain's imperial glory, her family was based in Egypt where her adored father worked, and she and her brother and sisters were sent 'home' to attend school. The journeys back and forth took five days, and although not the eldest, she was the one who took charge. At the age of sixteen a telegram told her of her father's sudden death, and two years later she lost her mother too.

Eileen struggled for a few years but when she married Andrew Combe, a distinguished RAF officer, her future seemed set. She bore him five children and was happy and content to bring them up, even among the falling bombs of wartime London. Andrew however was becoming distant and domineering, absorbed by his duties and obsessed with Moral Rearmament, which was a rather rigid and patriarchal spiritual practice to which Eileen did not relate. After the war Andrew, now a Wing Commander, was posted to the RAF base in Iraq. There they met Peter Caddy. Andrew began to cultivate him, seeing in him a potential candidate for Moral Rearmament. Peter did not let on that he was involved in his own, very different, spiritual practice, but often came to visit when passing through in the course of his duties. Eileen found him considerate, interesting and articulate, very different from Andrew. Then came the day when he very excitedly told her that, on a mountain top near Jerusalem, he had heard an inner voice telling him that she was his other half! Eileen laughed at him. They were both married to other people, and she had five children, to boot!

Andrew was posted back to Britain, and Eileen went ahead of him with the children to set up their house. Peter announced he would accompany her, and although her plane was overloaded, managed to board it at one of the stops en route. After a few weeks in England, Eileen was still on her own with the children when Peter invited her to have dinner with him and his wife Sheena. At the last minute, Sheena suffered a migraine headache and so Peter took Eileen out on his own. Quite suddenly, Eileen fell blissfully, ecstatically in love with Peter. Contrite, she wrote to Andrew, asking for an amicable separation. Bitter, Andrew returned to Britain, took charge of their house and forbade her any contact with her children. Faced too with her family's hostility, Eileen could hardly stop crying. How could she, a deeply conventional woman, have got herself into this mess?

Sheena seemed strangely undisturbed by her husband's new relationship and, in an attempt to distract Eileen from her grief, they took her to visit Glastonbury, England's holiest place. Eileen had never felt drawn to organised religion, but from childhood on she had wanted to know more about God. Now she began to pray, talking to Him as if He were a person. As she prayed, she heard a voice speaking inside her head: "Be still and know that I am God." The voice went on, "You have taken a very big step in your life. But if you follow my voice all will be well. I have brought you and Peter together for a very special purpose, to do a specific work for Me. You will work as one, and you will realise this more fully as time goes on. There are few who have been brought together in this way. Don't be afraid, for I am with you."

Eileen thought she was going crazy but Peter and Sheena were convinced that God had truly spoken to her. Eileen's thoughts kept turning to the Ten Commandments. The word 'adultery' plagued her. Why should He speak to a woman who had left her husband and children to 'live in sin' with another man? Peter now said that Sheena should be her teacher, as she had been his, but Eileen was deeply suspicious, sure that beneath her willingness, Sheena must be jealous and would try to take Peter away from her. Peter returned to the Middle East, leaving her in Sheena's charge. Sheena was a strong and powerful woman and Eileen was terrified of her.

Sheena had a mission in life: to transform the world through love. Increasing numbers of people came to her in their search for spiritual truth, but though she helped others, Eileen never felt her love. Though Sheena taught her to distinguish between God's voice and the other voices that intruded on her meditations, she was increasingly curt and cruel, criticising Eileen for not putting God first and insisting on perfection in everything, for that was God's way. Sheena was often ill, and Eileen became her nurse and maidservant. With no money and shunned by her family, Eileen could see no way out. Her few happy times were when Peter came home on leave, but when she complained about Sheena, he always replied that Sheena's way was the right way. Eventually her worst fear was realised. Sheena announced that Eileen was too dependent on Peter and it was because of him that she was not putting God first. They must not see each other for a while. Eileen was appalled, but Peter accepted Sheena's decision cheerfully.

Eileen took a live-in job baby-sitting, and now, when Peter came on leave, he stayed in another part of London. Nonetheless, they had a chance meeting in Battersea Park and began seeing each other. Soon Eileen found herself pregnant. For her, an illegitimate child was the ultimate sin against society but Peter and Sheena were delighted. Sheena told her that she herself had conceived a child by Peter, but had miscarried: "Of course, this baby you're going to have is the one I should have had." Eileen was silent, feeling only a great distaste.

The baby Christopher was born and for a while Eileen and Peter were together and she was blissfully happy. Then he had to leave for the Middle East and Eileen was persuaded to take Christopher to see Sheena, who instantly fell in love with him. The next few months are a horrid blur in Eileen's life. Sheena took charge of Christopher and refused to let Eileen see him. "You're not fit to be a mother," she kept saying. Peter who, at Sheena's direction, had resigned from the RAF and taken a job in Ireland as a cook, was no help at all. "He'll be quite safe with her," he told Eileen. "She told me that she'll keep him until you've learned to put God first in your life." Bitter and resentful, the voice in her head now silent and its words of comfort unheard, Eileen decided to end that life. She got hold of a bottle of sleeping pills and made ready to turn on the gas oven. Just then the front door bell rang. It was her brother Paddy.

Paddy was visiting town on business and had 'just happened to drop by'. He persuaded Eileen to come with him to Andrew's brother's farm where her children were staying. For a few short days there was a joyful, tearful reunion. Then Peter showed up one morning, gaunt, dishevelled (he had spent the night in a hedgerow), his hair turned white. His voice was choked with tears as he begged Eileen to come back with him. "I can't fulfil God's plan without you. We have to be together or both our lives will be a complete waste." Eileen extracted a promise that they would indeed be together and nowhere near Sheena, and to her children's great distress, she went with him. Now she heard her voice again, but its tone was stern. She was told that she had made a very big mistake and had indeed held up the spiritual work. It would now take longer to reunite with her family in love and harmony. Her lessons were obedience and patience. Eileen resolved to learn them so that she would never have such a heartrending experience again.

One would think this experience would see the end of trauma, but no! Eileen's second child Jonathan was born and after a little while Peter persuaded her to reconcile with Sheena and take the children to visit her where she was living on the island of Mull off the west coast of Scotland. At first, lodged in a cottage with mutual friends, all went well, but when the friends left, relations soured rapidly. Sheena left in a fury, stealing Christopher away and leaving Eileen in an isolated bothy with a peat hearth for heat and cooking, no running water and no money. Through the winter months she endured the worst time of her life, and might have starved but for a crofter's simple-minded son who brought her food and occasionally, what a blessing, a few lumps of coal! Peter could find no better job than as a door-to-door salesman, and sent her a little money when he could. Gradually, Eileen felt a change begin. Her blessings were indeed few, but she began to count them: the baby Jonathan; her simple-minded friend; the food; the coal; the plentiful peat; letters from Peter. She heard her voice, full of concern and comfort again.

Her vigil ended when Peter appeared on Christmas Day with a chicken

*affix*
*stamp*
*here*

to:

FINDHORN PRESS
305a The Park
Findhorn
Forres IV36 3TE
Scotland, Great Britain

FINDHORN Press

Tel 01309 690582 / Freephone 0800 389 9395
Fax 01309 690036
e-mail info@findhornpress.com
http://findhornpress.com

Thank you for choosing this book. We appreciate your interest and support.

If you would like to receive our full catalogue of books and other inspirational material, please fill in this card and mail it to us.

❑ Please send book and music catalogue (you can also consult our list on the web at findhornpress.com)

❑ Please send information about the Findhorn Foundation in Scotland (alternatively, see their website at findhorn.org)

Please write your name and address here *(please PRINT)*

What is your email address? ____________________

ready for roasting. They went back to the mainland with Jonathan. Sheena, unprompted, returned Christopher, and soon Peter was offered a job as manager of Cluny Hill Hotel in Forres. There he was shown two dark, dingy rooms and told these were the manager's quarters. Appalled, he sought Eileen's guidance. Her voice told her that the whole success of the venture depended on the health and well-being of the manager and they were to have the best rooms available, not the worst. So, despite his superior's baffled opposition, Peter moved his family into a suite on the first floor, one which had a sitting room with large bay windows overlooking the garden, two bedrooms and a luxurious bathroom. Now Eileen came into her own. She was Peter's mainstay, relaying her voice's guidance to help him plan ahead wisely, solve such day-to-day problems as what to do when the chef was drunk in the middle of a posh banquet and refusing to serve another meal ("Give him another drink"), and eventually raise the hotel to four-star status.

Another son was born and Eileen devoted herself to raising their three children. When Peter was transferred south to manage the Trossachs Hotel, she moved with him, then back north when he was fired, and so to the cramped caravan in the Findhorn Bay Caravan park. She was the calm at the centre of the storm. Always her guidance assured her that all was very, very well, and gave practical advice on how to deal with the day-to-day problems of raising a family of five on National Assistance. She tackled the toughest tasks without complaint. Sometimes she seemed a little bit more than human. Her friend Joanie related how they would go to the seashore even in freezing weather to collect seaweed for the garden, having read that it made good compost. One morning Eileen cut her hand on a sharp shell. The wound was deep and the blood flowed freely. Muttering, "I don't have time for this," Eileen stared at the cut. As Joanie watched amazed, the blood flow stopped. When they got back to the car with their sacks of seaweed, there was only the faintest line of a scar.

Eileen's problem was how to meditate in the cramped space of the caravan. In desperation she turned within and was told, "Why don't you go down to the public toilets? You will find perfect peace there." She always wrote down her guidance, full of comfort and practical advice, and soon friends were asking for copies. Demand grew and a little book was compiled, duplicated on a superannuated Gestetner. This brought in some money; just as well, for Peter's National Assistance had been terminated.

People came to see the garden and a few stayed. The Community was beginning to grow and Eileen's guidance was its foundation. For the first years she gave out its detailed directions for each day's work, and then she was told to give it out no more. The Community must learn to go within and learn to find its own guidance. There would be many ups and downs resulting but Eileen learned to remain detached, secure in the knowledge that all mistakes would turn into fruitful learning experiences. For some time now she had been making contact with the children she had had with Andrew and gradually the breaches were healing, but also, imperceptibly, a gulf was widening between her and Peter. He was in demand to give workshops abroad, and there he met women, very attractive women. Eileen was determined to save the marriage and they sought guidance from close friends. They were told that from being two halves of one whole, they were to become two wholes. Peter was to develop the Mary principle of love and understanding while Eileen was to take on the more masculine roles of leadership, will and wisdom. Then came the day when Peter told her that he was in love with a woman he had met in Hawaii. Eileen's rage knew no bounds and Peter withdrew still further.

In 1982 Peter wrote saying that he wanted to remarry. At first, Eileen's feelings were of disapproval, but after asking in meditation for God's grace, she was able to sincerely bless Peter in his new life. She felt more disapproval when Peter told her that his new wife Paula was going to bear their son Daniel, but nonetheless asked if she could visit them while on a workshop tour of California where they were living. It was a smooth and loving visit and Eileen marvelled at the irony – here she was, 65 years old, travelling the world to give talks and workshops, while Peter stayed at home changing nappies (diapers in USA). She realised later that it would have been impossible for her to have grown spiritually if she had remained with Peter – and it would have been impossible for Peter too.

Eileen has continued to live in the Community that she helped to found. Her eightieth birthday was graced by the presence of all her eight children, with many grandchildren and their wives and husbands, even a few 'greats' among them. It has come about as her guidance foretold: she and Peter would accomplish their task – to found a Community that would ground Light on the planet – and she would be reconciled with all her family.

Of Eileen's many words of guidance, two are constant in my heart: "To see the best in everyone and everything;" and to "Start the day by giving thanks." The message continues, " Realise that you are mightily blessed and that My blessings are being poured down upon you all the time. It does not matter how ungrateful you were yesterday; what matters is what your attitude is now. Leave the past behind." It was on Mull, when she had so little but began nonetheless to count her blessings and be grateful, that life changed for her. Her autobiography *Flight into Freedom and Beyond* tells more of her story.

*Exercise*

*Think over Eileen's story. Are there any aspects that are relevant to your life? Choose one and meditate on it awhile. Ask how you could use it for your health and happiness and service to the planet. Write down your insights.*

Eileen has this to say about unconditional love in her book *Divinely Ordinary, Divinely Human*, compiled by Dr. David Platts:

"I have learned that if we love solely from the emotional level, then we consciously or unconsciously are expecting something in return. Our love is then conditional, and is often possessive, indulgent, needy or sentimental. As long as we function principally from the emotional level, we are a slave to our own emotions, a puppet on the strings of our own emotions, in one emotional melodrama or soap opera after another.

"When we function from the level of unconditional love, recognising and giving thanks to the divinity within as the source of this divine love, we begin to know the meaning of freedom, and we are no longer tied up in knots emotionally.

"How few of us function from this level! When we do, how often we are misunderstood by those people who function principally from the emotional level! How complicated relationships become when they can be so simple and straightforward! All the more reason for us to change our outlook, our whole way of thinking if necessary, and so help those around us to change their way of thinking.

"I have learned that unconditional love does not come all at once. It starts in small ways and then grows one step at a time. Its benefits are enormous.

"Life is more abundant and fulfilling when we choose unconditional love as the primary principle which guides us. It is a deliberate choice we can make, one which serves us, everyone around us and the very planet itself. We transform the world as we transform ourselves with the power of unconditional love."

*Exercise*

*Ask to be shown some small way in which you can start to give unconditional love. When the answer comes, write it down and check from time to time on how you're practising it.*

---

# 7. The Appropriateness of Unconditional Love

"I do perceive here a divided duty."

*[William Shakespeare]*

It is time to revisit David Spangler's discussion of appropriate and unconditional love. Would it not have been appropriate for the White Christ, when he appeared to me at the end of my Viking incarnation, to have dealt with me somewhat differently? If he could not, of his nature, condemn me to the pit everlasting, perhaps he should have given me a lesson to treat his faithful more respectfully. This is where we see the divide between the physical and the spiritual. Appropriate love belongs to the physical. If my daughter complains of a headache and tells me she can't go to school, do I say, "Oh, you poor dear! What a pity that you're going to miss that test. It was important, wasn't it? Just lie back and I'll get you a light breakfast and a nice cup of tea," or do I say, "Wait while I get the thermometer. Oh, your temperature's normal! A headache won't stop you doing that test. Get up now or you'll miss the bus." The first option might be mistaken for unconditional love, but it's more like unconditional hate because it teaches the wrong lessons. At the very least, it's irresponsible, which is not far removed from hatred. The second option is appropriate. Where then is the place for unconditional love in that scenario? Probably in a warm kiss and a cuddle before she leaves for the bus. Actions speak louder than words.

The human is both physical and spiritual. In the Kingdom of God, where we belong, there is no evil. It's not even conceived of. That is why *A Course in Miracles* can say, "God's justice is mercy." Our karma and consequent decisions over the course of repeated lives will help us change our 'mistakes' into opportunities for fresh and wholesome creations. Hence it is appropriate to give unconditional love on the spiritual level because karma takes care of our trash. On the physical level we must be more discriminate in our giving. On that level, the White Christ's appropriate response to my Viking deeds was to allow me to fulfil their karma. I will revisit those deeds, work through them and heal them, and in doing so, new, undreamed-of creations and possibilities will arise, both for me and for those with whom I interact. One of the titles accorded to Jesus Christ is 'The Lord of Karma', because he is the only human to have lived a life that incurred no karma; in doing so, he won the grace to change its conditions for others. This grace may be what many people rely on, the idea that we can be changed 'in the twinkling of an eye', to be raised from our gross materialistic state and made into shining spiritual lights. It may well be our only recourse, but it's what William Blake disparagingly called "creeping into heaven by the back door." The front door is open and the way there is by unconditional love.

It is our task and joy to spiritualise matter and, as I suggested we do with the reluctant child, so with every situation that calls for appropriate loving we should look for the chink that opens into the unconditional variety. Love transforms and unconditional love transforms unconditionally. The opening may be surprising, and often is. Spirit loves new opportunities and can be very playful, even appear mischievous, for it knows that the grace of God is all-encompassing, and that all is always very, very well. This was the spirit of discovery that animated the *devas* – the angelic beings that hold the forms of plant species – whom Dorothy Maclean contacted and asked to help in the garden. We can read about this co-creation in *The Findhorn Garden*. They had never before engaged in conscious co-operation with humans and were intrigued to find out what the results would be. One result was that 40 lb. (16 kg.) cabbage!

Sometimes such spiritual promptings may appear offensive to outsiders. Alexandra David-Neel tells the story of a young Tibetan woman who went to draw water from the river. An old lama with a very saintly reputation was sitting by the stream, and in a field across the water two donkeys were copulating. Quite suddenly, the lama began to assault the young woman. She fought him off, for she was much stronger than he, but frightened at the change in the holy man, ran off to tell her mother. Her mother replied that the lama would have had a good reason for his behaviour, and she should go back and let him do whatever he wanted. Abashed, she returned, only to be told that she was too late. "I had no carnal desire for you, but was attempting a deed of mercy and compassion." The abbot of a nearby monastery had just passed away and, with his clairvoyant sight, the old lama had seen the houseless soul attracted to the copulating donkeys. He had wanted to offer an alternative. "Alas," he ended, "because of your stupid resistance, the soul of that ancient and respected lama will now be born in the body of an ass!"

The young woman, had she allowed conception to occur, would have lived an honoured and comfortable life as the mother of the new abbot, for it is the Tibetan custom, when a chief lama dies, to search for his new incarnation and to bring the young child to the monastery where he will resume his old status when he is grown. The deceased abbot should have known better than to head straight for the first warm and inviting grotto that opened to him (which, apparently, is how receptive wombs appear in the after-life). Alexandra David-Neel comments that sometimes human souls appears to regress through their successive incarnations, instancing some abbots whose originals had been most saintly and inspiring men, but presently were leading materialistic and hedonistic lives. On the other hand, because time does not exist outside the concrete, physical realm, the true, evolutionary succession of incarnations may differ from the chronological one.

The example of the Tibetan lama may appear repugnant to the western mind. Jesus may provide a more acceptable example of how spirit may guide us to act in opposition to society's laws and morals. You remember how he assaulted the moneychangers, prototype of modern bankers, at their place of business in the precincts of the Temple, overturning their tables, scattering their coinage, and driving them forth with a whip? Today, here in the West, he would have been hauled up before a court of law on multiple charges: assault with violence; felonious trespass; violation of a sacred precinct; terrorism; any prosecutor worth his salt could have thought up a dozen more. In the USA he would have got at least thirty years. Europe, not so inclined to fawn on capitalists, would have been more lenient, but not by much. It's chastening to reflect that, in Jesus' eyes, prostitutes like Mary of Magdala who "had loved much" were acceptable, but banking types were not.

To prepare ourselves for unconditional love, we don't have to forgive ourselves or others and engage in umpteen sessions of psychotherapy, useful though that may be for sorting out relationship issues. For unconditional love we can go straight for the gold. We can look for the centre of our being where spirit resides and may do this in meditation. There are many ways to practice this. Very much worth reading is Darren Main's *The Findhorn Book of Meditation.* Eileen Caddy advises to find a quiet place and time where you know you will be undisturbed, settle yourself but not so comfortably that you drop off to sleep, and go within. You may wish to set aside a regular space in your house for this sole purpose, perhaps with a little altar and a candle ready. Some teachers advise you to watch your passing thoughts, all the time disengaging yourself: 'I am not that thought, nor that one', and so on, until eventually you reach a place that is absolutely still and undisturbed. I find it simpler to go to the place in myself that is already calm and still – it usually seems to be at the back of my head – and let it lead me where it will. And then rest. I may close my eyes or watch the passing scene, it doesn't matter. The 'I am that I am' is at peace. Soon the feeling of joy and love creeps in and becomes all-sustaining.

How pleasant, and how self-serving! Unconditional love is not real until it is given to another. The hard part is to take that moment of joy, peace and love (however long it lasts, it's still only a moment) out into the busy world and give it appropriately to whatever is first available, human, animal, vegetable or mineral. And then to the next, and the next and so on. It's important not to delay or miss out, for the impulse may dwindle. With use it becomes stronger. The love may be a simple thought, an unspoken blessing bestowed on a passer-by or a blossoming tree, some small change given to a homeless man (what matter that he drinks it if it gives him some fleeting pleasure), a kiss for one's lover, all that matters is to pass the energy onward. It will return a hundredfold.

For me this is the most important part of the lesson: that I will only find my God in the other person. Meditation gives me such wonderful experiences that it's hard to believe they are insufficient. But when I see love shining in another's eyes – love for me, for another, for God, it matters not – that's when I see the Christ.

*Exercise*

*Settle yourself as indicated above and go within. Give yourself enough time to go deep and find your centre. When you feel that deep peace, rest there and be still. Afterwards, as you go out in the world, let your blessings flow. Set a time aside for daily meditation. Write down your insights.*

*If you cannot find your centre, do not worry. Just ask that it be shown to you when you are ready. It will happen. Continue to practise meditation daily. Write down your insights.*

*PART TWO*

# RELATIONSHIPS

"May I behold you with the eyes of Christ
and see my perfect sinlessness in you."

*[A Course in Miracles]*

# 8. REINCARNATIVE INFLUENCES

"You are part of My infinite plan."

*[Eileen Caddy]*

Conventional wisdom says that we are born *tabula rasa*, that is, our minds at birth are like a blank sheet on which our genetic inheritance and upbringing will write our behavioural patterns. In his poem *Intimations of Immortality*, William Wordsworth says otherwise:

"Our birth is but a sleep and a forgetting:
The Soul that rises with us, our life's Star
Hath had elsewhere its setting,
And cometh from afar:
Not in entire forgetfulness,
And not in utter nakedness,
But trailing clouds of glory do we come
From God, who is our home."

He might have truthfully added that those clouds contain a few thunderheads, but that would have spoilt the poem. This is the third factor, besides genes and upbringing, that goes into our make-up: the story of our former lives, housed and still living in the Soul (because we are immortal, right?). Recent studies and anecdotes indicate that babies in the womb have quite a high degree of consciousness, so we may say that the essence of our incarnated history is built into the foetus, along with our DNA. Upbringing overwrites what's already there but won't erase it, though it will modify behaviour, which is all that secular society cares about.

Those personalities with whom we have had unresolved issues in past lives can affect us quite powerfully in the present. Judy Hall has written the delightful book *Deja Who?* which goes in some detail into the mechanism of reincarnation. One reason for doubting the principle is that people's past life recollections tend to relate to the famous. It's been said that if all the reincarnations of King Arthur and Anne Boleyn were gathered together, they'd populate a city! Judy Hall tells us that each individual soul is part of a group soul, and that of a larger group soul, and so on, getting larger, until we arrive at the group soul of Humanity. We share the experiences of our group souls, and particularly if they are archetypes like King Arthur and Anne Boleyn, we can identify with them quite powerfully.

I had some experience of this with Peter Caddy, the co-founder of Findhorn, whom you met earlier. I have told how our personal relationship was strained, and though most people were happy to embrace him, my attitude was one of wary caution. During all my time at Findhorn I was unable to overcome my reserve, and it was not until years later, when I was living in Florida, that I began to get a clue what it was all about. The *Mary Rose* Exhibition had come to Tallahassee. The *Mary Rose* had been the flagship of King Henry VIII's fleet. The King and his court were watching as, flags flying, refitted with a new upper deck and heavier armament, she left harbour to lead the English fleet to do battle with the French, whose ships were lying off the Isle of Wight. Suddenly, a gust of wind took her and she capsized. In two minutes she had foundered. Some 800 crew were lost. In the 1980s the wreck was located under several feet of bottom mud and, with much effort, all that was left of the hull was raised and many artefacts recovered, a time capsule of Tudor England. As I wandered through the exhibition, I came upon a life-sized waxwork of the King, not as he is usually depicted, old and stout, but as he was in his athletic younger days. I found myself looking at Peter Caddy!

Limitless Love and Truth, in one of his transmissions to David Spangler, said that Peter had been prepared for his task at Findhorn over many lifetimes. And I remembered hearing that a psychic had told Peter that he was a reincarnation of King Henry. It began to fit, even to the number of his wives. Henry had six, Peter five, plus one serious liaison. The next clue was in the Tower of London. I knew that one of my first wife's ancestors had been executed there, but that did not explain my discomfort as I was shown around. The yeoman warder who was our guide made me the butt of his sarcastic wit – I believe they are all retired regimental sergeant majors – and I felt helpless, unable to put him in his place. I even tipped him at the end. Finally I read a book about, yes, you guessed, Anne Boleyn! She had had a musician in her little court, a lute player named Smeaton. When Henry fell out of love with Anne and she had produced no male heir, her enemies conspired to have her put to death. Led by the ruthless Thomas Cromwell, who stood to gain power and position by her demise, they accused her of adultery. A number of her friends were arrested as accomplices, together with the lute player. He was the only one without noble connections and Cromwell interrogated him first, under torture. He admitted to the crime.

They all died of course. I identify with that lute player, with a name so similar to the one I now bear. My friends twig me for my aversion to music and I have always had a problem with authority, though constantly dealing with it or serving it. My heart sags with shame at that poor man, dooming all with a false confession. One can always have another life, but dignity and honour, once lost, are hard to regain. The torturers must have been very hard on him, the commoner who had been so buoyed up with hopes of advancement and was now in despair, an easy mark. And that yeoman warder, he was one of them! He had learned little of love and compassion in the years between.

All fantasy maybe, but it explains my feelings towards Peter Caddy. I never had a chance in his lifetime to talk with him about it. And I think he would have said, correctly, that the transaction was not relevant to our present lives. "Get over it," might have been his reaction, based on his experience, for he would have had his own karma to deal with. And, just think, if he had been Henry VIII, what he accomplished: freeing the English Church to pursue its spiritual growth independent of Rome, releasing the wealth of the monasteries to fuel the great enterprises of succeeding centuries, maintaining his usurping dynasty, presiding over a renaissance of learning, founding the fleet that in his daughter's reign would defeat the Spanish Armada, and taking England out of the Middle Ages to the threshold of modern times! Tens of thousands were swept up in the tides of those great events and details like an unhappy lute player get lost in the crush. If one with such a far history was designated to co-found Findhorn, the place must be more important than appears to the outer eye.

Does knowledge of past life experiences help overcome difficult relationships in the present? I think that depends on how you deal with the knowledge. It may not help at all to know that the person you dislike so intensely is the one who killed your lover in your last lifetime but one, particularly if, like that yeoman warder, he hasn't changed much in the meantime. However, there are ways to release the experience, some better than others.

Some qualified psychotherapists use regression hypnosis to resolve otherwise intractable behavioural issues, and in one report I read that, in five per cent of cases treated, the relevant trauma had happened in a prior lifetime. Although it is possible to perform regression hypnosis on oneself, or gain snippets of past life experiences through a process known as Rebirthing, I would always advise going to a qualified psychologist if you have issues to resolve. It's all too possible for experiences to surface that you need help to deal with. That is one reason why you forgot them.

This is why I have never used regression to heal my relationship with Peter Caddy. Frankly, I have been scared. I do not want to meet that yeoman warder again, even in my imagination. The pleasure he took in random cruelty was too unsubtle. And the proud King who gave the orders, whose passionate outpourings gave us *Greensleeves* but then turned to a murderous hatred where human beings were merely flies to be crushed. Oh no! My grief has been too alive within me: grief for proffered favours turned to accusations; for doomed hopes; for friendships suddenly grown cold; most of all for the poor soul ground down by pain, who betrayed himself and everyone.

Writing this account has made me realise that the experience has had a much greater influence on my present life than I thought. It really needs to be exorcised and I have now been shown a way to do it safely and without the unpleasantness of hypnotic regression. The method is to hold the events in one's mind's eye, confront each character in full consciousness, look within them to see where they are coming from, and feel their agony and pain as well as your own. For they felt the pain in their inner being, even while their outer was acting contrary. I find my feelings change even as I work through the process, and I have been able to ground in my personality the same unconditional love for Peter Caddy that my Higher Self extends, replacing mere appropriateness. I recognise that whatever karma he may have acquired in respect of the 'me' known as Smeaton, he had redeemed it by offering me unparalleled opportunities for growth in this present life. I can even include that yeoman warder who is still so very unhappy! And that is my purpose here, to bring unconditional love into my physical life.

*Exercise*

*Read over what you have written in your journal. Have your insights and understanding changed over time? Where are the changes leading you? Write down your observations.*

---

# 9. The Divided Personality

"Everything that takes place in your life
happens because of your consciousness."

*[Eileen Caddy]*

I have suggested that we differentiate between occasions for appropriate and unconditional love, but we still have to ask how well do we know ourselves? Surely we should know who it is that is supposed to be doing the loving. Are we really the integrated soul we like to imagine, except of course for those occasional upsets brought on by too much celebration or a bad day at the office? Up to now we have distinguished only between the Higher Self and our ego nature. I have suggested that the latter is our normal operating level, and as such it is the one that judges between occasions for appropriate and unconditional loving in the concrete world, and seeks to ground unconditional love in itself and apply it more widely.

However, the time has come to be rather more sophisticated and to do so I want to take a rather different approach to our psyche.. The human being is such a very complex entity that it presents a different aspect dependent on what you are looking for. The spiritual and psychological views of the human being are quite different. I want us to look at ourselves as beings capable of giving and receiving unconditional love, which is similar to the spiritual approach but rather more focused. I believe that if we understand ourselves from that point of focus, it will be easier to understand the competing claims of other aspects of our being which are running interference.

Let's start with the proposition that we are a combination of Body, Soul and Spirit. This was standard teaching till about the Seventh Century CE when the Church hierarchy realised that perception of Spirit would be lost as we entered more deeply into the age now passing, which they called the Age of Iron (often known by its Indian name, Kali Yuga). Seeing no point in teaching the incomprehensible, they decided to concentrate on the two aspects of which people remained aware, Body and Soul. In present time, perception of Soul has also been lost and we are reduced to Body, witness the performer Madonna, the current icon.

The original spiritual teaching remains valid however. We are still composed of Body, Soul and Spirit. It is part of Findhorn's purpose to help us regain perception of the last two and recognise the aspect of each that is embedded in the others. Spirit is pure unconditional love, and freedom is the air it breathes. Spirit is unity, in that all its degrees are united in the Godhead, which is One. The degree closest to Soul and communicating with it is the Higher Self. Soul has been variously described, but it may be conceived for our present purposes as a combination of sensation, emotion, affect, desire, behaviour, beliefs, principles, strengths and weaknesses, all the things that go to make up the personality. The Soul's purpose is to be infused with Spirit, and Spirit uses the Body to teach the Soul. Every time we think we've learned something, we get tested on it. The Body we are getting to know, and here is not the place to discuss its various aspects, and the meridians and chakras that are the expressions of Soul and Spirit within it. Other books tell you about those.

The concept of Soul as personality differs from the popular meaning, which likes to see only that aspect that has risen, or will rise, to divine awareness. To make for easier understanding, I will use 'Soul' (capitalised) henceforth to mean only that part of our personality that is growing into divine awareness. If 'soul' is used in lower case letters, it will have the usual meaning, as in, "She's a good soul." I will also use 'personality' in the commonly accepted sense, meaning all the aspects and behaviours, expressed or unexpressed, of which we are composed. 'Ego' has been given several meanings, which make for confusion, and I will discard that word altogether. For our purposes therefore, we may say that we are composed of Body, personality (of which Soul is a part), and Spirit.

Now we need to look at those parts of the personality that are not 'Soul', and which I suggest have a quite different agenda. In his great play-poem *Faust*, the German philosopher-statesman-poet Goethe has his hero encounter those aspects in an actual being. They combine to manifest first as a black poodle, then as a human-like person who calls himself Mephistopheles. "*Ich bin der Geist der stets verneint*," (I am the spirit which always says no!), he announces. I will follow Goethe's lead by giving the name Mephisto to the interference aspects of my personality, and ask you to note that he combines Luciferic and Satanic characteristics, both the drive towards indulgence and the drive to organise, make rules, be rigid. Often they oppose each other, sometimes act together, but they work always in opposition to the Soul. Nonetheless they are part of our being, because both Satan and Lucifer were involved in our original entry into a physical body. I suppose this is why the Church propounded the doctrine of 'original sin'. But it's not something to feel guilty about, it's just part of being human, of our mission to spiritualise matter, which involves the redemption of both Satan and Lucifer.

There is still one entity missing from the caste of characters that are part of our make-up. This is the Moral Self, the one that makes the decisions from among the competing claims advanced by Mephisto and the Soul. The Moral Self is distinct from the Higher Self, which is Spirit and our guide on life's pathways. The Moral Self is the essence of our being, good and bad, and the decisions it makes are based on its experience and inclinations. Those decisions and consequent behaviours determine the nature of the Moral Self, which follows us from life to life.

Mephisto secretly wants our destruction, and he has his own version of unconditionality: it is unconditional hatred, expressed in our addictions to drugs, alcohol, sex and whatever, or in Faust's case to the pursuit of knowledge and experience, for which, incidentally, Heaven forgave him. On the other side, as it were, stands the Soul that is aligned with the Higher Self. How often do we hear something like an argument going on inside our head? "You know you'd really like to do that!" and the response, "No, it feels wrong and the outcomes look too doubtful, I think I'll do something else." And in the end the Moral Self, which stands in the middle, will make the decision, for it has free will to choose – and responsibility too for it is immortal, enduring between incarnations and incurring karma.

The Soul is wise and prescient, leaning on the Higher Self and advising us always for the highest good. This does not always correspond with our immediate and material benefit, which is what interests Mephisto. Sometimes, our choices in accordance with the Higher Self's guidance involve painful, even dangerous learning experiences. This annoys Mephisto considerably, for such initiatives are quite senseless within his rather limited frame of reference. He is importunate, thrusting himself forward to delay or deny healthy and propitious proposals and foster unhealthy ones. In contrast, the Soul is quiet and steadfast; in my mind, she is like the wise and capable daughter and Mephisto a bumptious son. If you have experience of either of them, you will have your own descriptions for them. Mephisto uses both the Luciferic and Satanic sides to his nature – flexibility and rigidity respectively – to gain his ends, which are to divert us away from any spiritual path, and incidentally cause us as much harm as possible. It is extremely unsettling to become aware of such hatred lurking near the centre of one's being.

I am proposing this model of the human being only in order to help us better understand our various reactions to occasions for unconditional love, either allowing it to be given and received, or offering something else, dismissal, revulsion or even hatred. We can use it to see how the different aspects of our nature play into our thoughts and actions and determine our moral stature. I am not suggesting the replacement of any of the psychological and spiritual models already current, only a complementary approach.

You may feel that I have gone too far in personifying the tempter part of ourselves, departing way beyond conventional thinking. I have made this choice deliberately because I feel the tempter part is necessary to the physicality of our human nature, but I really do not want to own it forever. Giving it a name that is not my own implies a degree of separation, which I hope will grow wider.

In some ways Mephisto is a pitiable character, as well as contemptible. His one aim is his human host's destruction, yet, like his diabolic masters, his being and purpose depend on us. No wonder his manifestations appear schizoid when they surface in those humans drawn by greed and a need for power. Some say that he always speaks first, thrusting himself forward, but I think this only holds good in everyday matters. An intuition or piece of guidance may very well come first, and then Mephisto will intervene, either advancing legions of objections to do with time, support and resources available, or if these do not serve, enthusiastically inflating the idea beyond bounds of practicality. He is ever ready to help us shoot ourselves in the foot, and the idea of unconditional love seems to him not only abominable but impossible.

Some of us are more mephistically inclined than others, but we all need to detect him whenever he appears, and then use our knowledge of him to redeem him. That's unconditional love, not for the being that he is now but for what he is in potential. Clement of Alexandria, a good heretic, said that even the Devil must be saved. That is already true of Lucifer, though some of his demons remain around. Our task is Satan, our creation, for whom we are responsible. There is a simple way to do this. When we are confronted with a decision where, even after meditation, the moral choice is unclear, we look at the options. Which is too much (excess)? Which is too little (lack)? Is there a middle path? That is likely to be the right one. Incidentally, middle does not mean dull. God seems to want us to live intensely, to experience life to the full.

Makes sense if it's true that God experiences Itself through us. That's why we have free will.

Sometimes we are facing a big decision and all the options seem evil. We are stuck on the horns of a dilemma. Then we summon our patience and perseverance and hang on, waiting till the last possible moment. It often happens that, all of a sudden, a new way opens up, taking us safely past the evils on either side. As we go, we cross a spiritual threshold and take some of those evils with us, redeeming and transforming them.

If we don't do this, Mephisto begins to infect the personality and taint the Moral Self. There is a painting by the mediaeval seer Hieronymus Bosch that shows two female deer, images of the personality, or soul as he would say, that are standing close beside each other. One is drinking from a polluted stream, the other from a pure, unsullied spring. This image has always been true, but I think that it has particular relevance to the present day. In this I follow Marko Pogacnik whose clairvoyance tells him that changes are happening on the etheric level of planet Earth and are working their way through to its physical level, affecting us too. At the moment, our stubborn thought forms, like the crusted cap formed on the summit of a dormant volcano, are holding up the process, so the changes, when they happen, may be catastrophic. One of LLT's transmissions to David Spangler foretells a separation of consciousness, and Pogacnik also sees this happening, relating it to the Biblical passages in Luke and Matthew:

"I tell you, in that night there shall be two men in one bed; the one shall be taken, and the other shall be left. Two women shall be grinding together; one shall be taken, and the other left. Two men shall be in the field; the one shall be taken, and the other left." (Luke 18:34–36)

Pogacnik suggests that the above passage is looking at the two personality or soul sides of a single person. The sides that are taken are travelling to the Kingdom of God. I theorise that the ones left behind may not notice much change, perhaps only that they can get on with business without the usual aggravating twinges of conscience! And that business may get pretty nasty. In a controversial book channelled by Princess Diana after her death, she suggests that if humankind does not take the heavenly path, we shall evolve into a technological civilisation with a multitude of attendant horrors of the 'star wars' type. Not Hell exactly, but certainly one of our own making. Admit it, the Mephisto part of us actually rather relishes the prospect, for it will ensure his continued existence. But then, he can't envision Heaven, except perhaps as serried ranks of haloed saints twanging harps. I remember watching a Footlight's Revue while up at Cambridge. There was a rather pretty but dispirited blonde holding up a lily, as in a Botticelli painting, singing how she was bored, forever singing praises to the Lord. That Byzantine court again, nurturing its odd idea of heaven. Actually, the few accounts we have suggest that Heaven has many levels and they are all exceptionally original, enjoyable and creative.

While Mephisto may look forward to the separation of consciousness, seeing it as his vindication, Pogacnik suggests that, on the contrary, the physical world will be transmuted and become the basis for an inter-galactic communications web. So the Devil is to be saved after all! This is in fact our karma, for by choosing to take on a physical body, we created him and are therefore responsible for him! This means that the personality sides 'left behind' will still be fulfilling a continuing divine purpose. I guess that this is the meaning of eternity, a constant exploration into God.

The concept of a separation of consciousness would also explain why St. Michael's messages, quoted in Marko's books, emphasise on the one hand that "no one shall be left behind," and on the other, the extreme urgency of relating and adapting to the current earth changes in order to lessen their violent impact on us, which rather indicates that some part of us may be left behind after all. I have the sense that Michael's *angst* is occasioned by the prospect of the separation of the evolutionary paths of the angelic realm and one part of humankind. He has been our guardian for countless aeons, not an easy task, and seeing us, like wilful teenagers, about to set off on our own, is a gut-wrenching prospect to which many parents will relate.

I have become aware of yet another possibility that has to do with the nature of time. Time is a construct of matter. Spiritual evolution, which is the purpose of reincarnation, takes place outside time. So although reincarnation takes place 'within time', it is not 'of time', supporting the idea that our spiritual progress is independent of chronology. In her book *Winged Pharaoh*, Joan Grant tells of a life in Egypt 5,000 years ago where her Soul appears considerably more advanced than in her accounts of herself in later incarnations. It may be that we have already achieved a far higher degree of spiritual perfection than our current status would suggest. This proposition suggests an elegant solution to the conflict between the lop-sided drive to evolve and the universe's need for balance. If the more highly evolved steps are balanced within time by the less evolved, then the highly evolved can accumulate outside of time until the whole process becomes top-heavy and tips over, so that a new cycle can begin.

*Exercise*

*To look at your Moral Self, think about past dilemmas in your life, the occasions when it was really hard to make a decision. Is there any pattern in the way you made the decisions? How do the outcomes look now? Is there any connection between how you made a decision and how the results turned out? Can you allow unconditional love to play into such thorny questions in the future? What practical steps will you take to ensure that it does? Go within for the answers. Later, write down your insights.*

# 10. The Conundrums of Love

"Learn to seek within for all the answers.
Take time to be still, and find the answer in the silence.
Never despair if it does not come immediately."

*[Eileen Caddy]*

Our Nearest and Dearest

There's a little gift shop in the fishing village near my beach cottage that sells signs to hang by your front door – you know, "Welcome" – that sort of thing. Quite a good seller is one that reads, "Friends welcome any time. Relatives by appointment." We choose our friends. Relatives, we may feel, are wished on us. By now we are probably getting to realise that the wishing is done by our Higher Self, which has chosen them as the learning experiences most necessary for our present lifetime. Our closest relatives most likely include some with whom we have quite heavy reincarnative issues. Other 'heavies' we will meet in the course of our life's journey. Yet, if we look around, we will also find those who are wise and supportive and guide us with a firm and gentle hand. If we are lucky, they will be our parents. So, now that we've sorted out who we really are in our divided journeying soul, shall we start with the easy relationships, like our parents, and brothers and sisters? You'll probably say, I'm joking, and yes, I am.

I am a parent several times over and I find it extremely hard to give my children unconditional love. It was part of my job to educate them and I can't stop myself having an agenda, even if unspoken: I want them to be healthy and happy certainly; to be successful maybe, but not as a Mafia boss or the selfish sort of CEO. So I put conditions on my loving and it becomes appropriate love, not unconditional. I have to confront the terrifying fact that it is when the child has fallen so far that they can fall no further that our love becomes unconditional, and I pray that never happens. But there is a healing power at work. There is a place in my Soul where unconditional love resides, ready for use, and in my imagination I can travel there and give my children that love without invoking catastrophe.

I can give my parents both appropriate and unconditional love. Appropriate for the life we lived together, taking joy in the fun we had and thoughts we shared, and grieving for misplaced expectations and opportunities, tempered with the realisation that I went along and share responsibility. We all did the best that we knew at the time. And I can give unconditional love to the part of them that is the Soul, pure, blameless and utterly loving; from mine to theirs.

*Exercise*

*Think about your parents. You may grieve for them, especially if they have passed on and you still have unresolved issues. Dismiss those thoughts and concentrate on the inner core of your love for them. Tears are OK. They help to cleanse the soul. Your love will bring them close to you, for they live on, just as you do. Talk to them, tell them how you love them; talk to them about the issues you'd like to resolve; be honest, say where you went wrong and where you think they did, and ask for forgiveness. And then feel the unconditional love that flows between you. Later, write down the thoughts that came to you.*

There's really no place like the nuclear family to give you an early experience of jealousy and competition. Later on in life you may find that climbing the ladder in large corporations, in politics, or even in the military, will engender the same feelings, but they will not be compounded and confused by the awful admonition to love those whom you may sometimes sincerely wish were dead. Twins aside, the spacing between births, the eldest child's sense of having lost its place as the focal point of parental love, the younger child's curiosity and tendency to disrupt the elders' activities, all make for degrees of anger ranging from irritation to outright hatred. It follows that, if we can overcome those feelings, there is no place like the nuclear family to evoke unconditional love.

We should not worry if love is not always the feeling on the surface of our minds. Family interactions are so frequent that disagreements are commonplace. But that's what they are, commonplace. The deep, abiding feeling is usually unconditional love. But sometimes things go the other way. Newspaper advice columns are full of complaints by one family member about another. The subject is often money or care for an ageing parent. The response given is usually the sort of pabulum that enables everybody to get on with life without disrupting their comfortable middle-class existence, attachment to which may have been the original cause of the problem

'Stuck' Relationships

Is there anyone in your life with whom you have a persistently bad relationship? Someone you just can't get through to? *A Course in Miracles* teaches us about the holy instant. It tells us that we are host to God and worthy of Him, not with any idea of arrogance but in humility. The holy instant is the result of our determination to be holy. We should not seek holiness but should let go and let God, who sees us as we are – already holy. When we feel that the holiness of our relationship with another is threatened, we should stop instantly and offer the Holy Spirit our willingness to exchange this instant for the holy instant we would rather have, repeating these words in our mind,

"I desire this holy instant for myself
That I may share it with my brother, whom I love.
It is not possible that I can have it without him, or he without me.
Yet it is wholly possible for us to share it now
And so I choose this instant as the one to offer to the Holy Spirit,
That his blessing may descend upon us, and keep us both in peace."

I find this invocation invaluable. It does not need the other's knowledge or consent, for we are joined in our relationship and either may do it for both. I can sense an objection arising, that this infringes on the free will of the other. The response of *A Course in Miracles* is contained in its Introduction, "Free will does not mean that you can establish the curriculum." The curriculum is contained within the will of God, which is peace and joy, and the invocation is consistent with that.

If I am too fraught to use the invocation at once, I use it later, focusing on the other person, feeling once again my emotions when the interchange was most intense and offering them to the Holy Spirit, for his particular gift is to bring good out of bad. The invocation will work even where there is active resentment and dispute, and also in those cases where a truce has been called but little or no communication is taking place. The last is more common than is realised, for it occurs whenever one or the other finds it necessary to avoid 'touchy' subjects.

*Exercise*

*Ask for the Holy Spirit's presence. If this idea is foreign to you, offer a prayer to the spirit, goddess or angel of Transmutation (the old alchemical idea of turning base metal into gold). Then think over your acquaintances. Is there one who consistently gives you difficulties, whom you can hardly talk to without your hackles rising? Concentrate on that person. Let yourself feel the emotions they arouse in you and offer all your feelings to the Holy Spirit (or whomever you invoked), while repeating the above prayer. Infuse your words with all possible desire.*

## Wives and Husbands

I am told that there was an Anglican priest in the last century who used to thunder from the pulpit, "There is more adultery in the marriage bed than anywhere." No, he wasn't referring to loving wives sneaking the milkman in for a quickie (husbands still find the illicit use of the home more difficult to arrange), he was referring to the derivation of the word 'adultery', which is 'sex without love'. That should give us pause.

Of course, there are problems with the meaning of the word 'sex', as evidenced by past difficulties in America's White House. I think the good priest was limiting the meaning to penetration, but if we interpret it more widely to include all cross-gender attraction (or same gender if homosexual), we can see that he was wrong. Eileen Caddy has said that since sex is part of our make-up, we should not be disturbed if we have sexual feelings for another who is not a committed partner. Whether we act on those feelings is quite a different matter. It is commonplace that sex has ruined many a good relationship. The same could be said of marriage.

The problem lies with the thought forms. These are a sort of atmospheric which surrounds us and which we imbibe, usually unconsciously. 'Marriage' carries a whole lot of baggage, like housewife, male provider, children, home. Sex has other baggage, like orgasm, fulfilment, domination and submission. If these thought forms don't fit with our life's path, there will be problems that require either that they be discarded or the relationship adjusted. Our life's path does not adjust, it is a given.

The major problem with the thought forms of both marriage and sex is the idea of possession. If we think we can or should possess our partner, we do not love unconditionally. And the opposite is true. This is beautifully illustrated in the story "Letting Go," told in the next chapter. Possessiveness leads to a culture where cheating, in American parlance, is endemic and leads to conflict. Europeans tend to refer to 'arrangements', so acknowledged as to be hardly hypocrisy, and condone them in each other as necessary to the social convenience of monogamy. My understanding of history and the lives that I have witnessed is that our life's path takes precedence over all contractual arrangements whatsoever. Our path may indeed include absolute faithfulness, but it will never lead us into hypocrisy.

## Conflicts of Love

One way to distinguish between appropriate and unconditional love is to ask if conflict is involved. If it is, the love is appropriate, not unconditional. Parental love offers a good example. I still think about an episode when I had the chance to learn to fly, literally for free, while at university. My internal conversation went like this:

Luciferic Mephisto speaking: "It's free, and flying is really glamorous, you know."

Satanic Mephisto intervenes: "You're pretty unsure of yourself. You may mess up in training and be a laughing stock. Perhaps you'll crash."

My Soul urges: "It's a wonderful opportunity for a completely new experience, and it could be very useful in the future. Go for it."

Later, my mother, speaking quite vehemently for her, "Oh, don't! I swear I'll die with fear if you try to do that."

My mother's *angst* decided me, and I did not learn to fly. My Soul, had I continued to consult it, would have said that it was a chance to overcome the low self-esteem that dogged me. It would have added that my mother's fears were her own business and I should not take responsibility for them, but my understanding had not evolved to be able to embrace that concept. Intuition does not work well in a vacuum. It works best when there is a framework into which it can insert its ideas, which is another reason for us to educate ourselves as widely as possible. Actually, I now believe that the Soul, knowing that we are immortal and that our nature is rooted in the divine source that is Love, does not even know about fear. "Perfect love casteth out fear," says the evangelist. Another maxim says that we invoke what we are afraid of. Pity that our culture tries to make us fear so much.

A more common source of conflict is parental or family urging to enter a particular business, trade or profession. This is when it becomes really important to know our life's path. It is always harder to disentangle yourself from a career after you have entered it than to come straight out immediately and declare that your true intention is elsewhere. The difficulty, at a young age, is to know what is our life's path. Still worth taking the risk, I say. When people come to me, stuck in an unfulfilling job and wanting to change but not knowing what to do instead, I ask them what fired their imagination when they were young. I suggest they go back in memory as far as they can reach and search among their unfulfilled desires. There, surely, they will strike gold, for we never forget what we truly want.

*Exercise*

*Think over your life. What is left undone? Is there still some project that fills you with desire? If so, make a note of it. It may be important later when we come to the Manifestation Exercise.*

# 11. EXPERIENCING UNCONDITIONAL LOVE

"Let me not to the marriage of true minds admit impediments
Love is not love which alters when it alteration finds"
*[William Shakespeare]*

Growing Up

A woman tells me her story of the love that alters not:

I have experienced unconditional love in many forms from a woman nearly twice my age. We came together first when I was in my vulnerable youth and in much need of tenderness and nurturing, and she, though mature in years, was facing emptiness and a great need for acceptance.

Initially our coming together was physical, me aged 16, she in her mid 40s, both of us starved for affection and recognition. After about a year, I left her for a man 12 years older than myself, and even though this hurt her immensely, she was there for me when it ended, helping me to deal with some serious issues I faced in that situation.

My rocky relationship and marriage to that man had lasted a total of seven years and during that time she and I had hardly spoken. I was ashamed and embarrassed that I had been attracted both physically and mentally to a woman. However, she was the one I went to when the marriage ended. Never did she reject or judge me for failing to nurture our friendship during those seven years.

We once again began a romantic, though long-distance, relationship that lasted a couple of years. I was in my youthful 20s, finishing college, and was not always faithful to her, dating and having a number of meaningless affairs. I always dreaded having to confess to her next day, knowing how much she would be hurt. She was indeed upset, but never rejected or judged me. She very much wanted my happiness, but knew we could never truly be together, for she was married and the scandal would have made our situation intolerable. And indeed, once again I found someone to be committed to long term and went through another period of my life avoiding contact with her. When that ended, she was there once again to help pick up the pieces, never judging or rejecting me.

I believe that over the course of our twenty-five year on-and-off-again relationship, she has been the one constant, solid foundation on which I could rely in time of need. She truly loves me unconditionally, never trying to change or mould me into something I am not, as parents sometimes do. She early taught me the meaning of unconditional love and she has always been my model, keeping me centred when making decisions about subsequent relationships.

Now I have found someone for whom I can feel the unconditional love she taught me. I enjoy this new person's soul and spirit, her mind and body. She fills me completely. I feel that she too loves me in the same way. She enjoys my company, we have fun together, she respects my interests and hobbies and she doesn't try to change my ways of thinking and doing. To be loved unconditionally is the most beautiful feeling, and when you didn't necessarily grow up experiencing it, you certainly recognise it and don't take it for granted!

## Receiving Love

My friend was lucky to learn unconditional love while still quite young. Mephisto's influence often makes it hard for us to receive love, for he fills us with a deep sense of unworthiness. We tend to dismiss the approbation of friends, believing we are being modest when we say, "Oh, I don't deserve that," when in fact we are disrespecting them. I even find it hard to accept my children's unconditional love, for there are ways in which I wish I had been a better parent. And yet I know, and have had many proofs, that despite all my mistakes, they love me unconditionally.

*Exercise*

*Think of a being that you know well, one who loves you unconditionally – spouse, friend, child or pet – then let yourself really feel that love. Bathe in it, bask in it, acknowledge it and return it. Then give thanks. Make a mental note to practise this whenever you're feeling low.*

Vulnerability

My stepdaughter Shaye, who is a TV producer and Southern born and bred, recently had to go into hospital. This is how she describes the experience, in her own words:

I guess it all started on a Thursday when I was at work typing, and I felt an unbelievable explosion of pain in my abdomen. I called the doctor's office and suggested a prescription.

"Oh, you don't want to take pills for that," they told me.

I said that I had been taking Ibuprofen for a headache for the past week or two.

"Oh no! You don't want to do that. You can put a hole in your stomach doing that. Your stomach's probably just irritated right now. Don't eat or drink anything for 4-5 hours and let your tummy rest. If it gets really bad, have us paged."

Back at home, I dealt with the pain for some twelve hours. Then I woke up my husband Stewart at about 3:30 in the morning. He took me to the hospital emergency room, and after many tests we found out I had a perforated ulcer – basically a hole in my intestine – and I needed emergency surgery. When they told me this, I got upset and started crying. I guess I had convinced myself it was just gas and hadn't realised how serious it was.

I went in for the operation and my husband was the last person I saw. He told me that he loved me and that I was going to be okay. When I came out of surgery, he was the first person I saw, standing right over my bed, rubbing my hair and still telling me that everything was going to be okay. I know I needed the assurance at the time.

I was in hospital for five nights and six days and Stewart spent every single day with me. And I know that visiting the hospital and seeing friends and loved ones there is really difficult – you chit-chat and whatever, but it's hard – seeing things that you really don't want to see. Yet Stewart stayed with me. He spent every waking moment with me, even though for the first couple of days I was fading in and out of consciousness from all the painkillers they had me on. I had a nasogastric tube in my throat and everything I swallowed – and I was able to swallow ice chips – went straight into my stomach and exited through a tube that came out of my nose and into a bucket-type-thingee. It was really disgusting and I tell ya, I was extremely miserable. Yet Stewart always stayed there with me, and told me that I would be okay, that I had just had surgery and this was part of it, not to worry, it would all just be a memory.

Eventually it came to a point when I could not talk. The tube irritated my throat so much that I had to write everything down. I was so crabby and so miserable, you have no clue. And Stewart stayed with me and never said, "Gee, you just need to calm down," or any of that stuff. He never was like that. Though I ended up having to use sign language and write things down, he kept so positive and loving about the whole thing. He was so supportive.

Once they took out the nasogastric tube and I was able to speak, I told him, "You know, I love you so much. I can't believe you've stayed with me throughout." And he said, "Well, I'm your husband, what do you expect? Of course I'm going to stay with you." It amazes me how natural this is for him. I guess that's what unconditional love is all about.

And I have to say that I don't know if I would have reacted in the same way. It's such a natural thing for him – I know his family is very loving and supportive – I think that's where he gets it from. I don't think I've ever felt that before in my life, that true, unselfish, unconditional love, coming from someone whom you know truly loves you. I know that my parents love me and they show me unconditional love, but this is the first person outside of some blood relative that has shown me that they truly care about me and love me. Stewart and I have only been married for a couple of years, but I know I will never forget this situation and I'll always, always have this in my mind – how he stayed with me and showed me that love that we all so desperately want and need in our lives – unconditional love – and how lucky am I to have found it.

## Healing

A friend tells me of the osteopath she goes to, how she feels unconditional love pouring through his hands. She describes him as a spiritually inclined human being who is totally nonjudgmental. When he lays his hands on her, she knows that the energy is coming from the heart centre. Tears run.

Physically and Mentally Challenged

My work as a massage therapist leads me among people whom society has variously categorised as 'handicapped', 'disabled', or in the old days, 'crippled'. Those who are verbal tell me that they prefer the word 'challenged'. They are of all ages, and for some, touch and taste are their only remaining senses. When I am with them, I try to tune in to the place where they are at, and work on the inner as well as the outer planes. I find, with few exceptions, that the more profoundly they are affected, the deeper, more serene and more loving is the place where they reside. Then the experience becomes even more fulfilling for me, because I get to go there too.

Staff at the facilities where some of these 'challenged' individuals live tell me that they too have this experience of their clients' radiating love. It is for that that they stay on despite poor pay and bad conditions. Some of the parents know this too and rejoice in the qualities that their child possesses. Others are attached to what they see as 'normal' and mourn the might-have-been star athlete or brilliant scholar: attached to what was never there, they cannot see the treasure that is. A few feel desperate guilt for what they have produced and turn their self-blame on everyone around. I feel very sorry for them. They do not want to hear about the incredible gift they have brought into the world: An innocent soul, without taint, willing to share its purity and love with those who are open. They remind me of C. S. Lewis' tale about the black dwarfs in his book *The Last Battle*. The dwarfs had refused to fight and, when the battle was over, the victors saw them seated in a gorgeous pavilion with a magnificent banquet spread before them; but the dwarfs could only see themselves seated on ill-smelling straw in a dank and gloomy stable with nothing to eat but rotten turnips.

It is a pity that some able-bodied people turn away from the physically and mentally challenged, saying that they cannot bear to look at them. All they can see are contracted bodies and disabled minds, but if they would look deeper, they would find the innocence and love that they are vainly seeking, and often behind it there is joy. In their real nature many of the challenged are like stars, come down to shine on earth.

### Challenged Love

I have a physically challenged friend who is severely spastic, but bright, eloquent and intelligent. She is married to a man more challenged than herself, non-verbal but whose articulations she can interpret. She has undergone more than a dozen painful surgeries for her various physical conditions, some of which have left her more physically affected than before. She has been hurt. Two of her brothers have died. All this pain, all these challenges, she has transmuted into a burning love for her husband, a love that is without hope of normal sexual consummation but nonetheless shines brightly.

He, poor man, is often in pain and continually frustrated that he can do so little to demonstrate how he returns his wife's love. Sometimes they quarrel, but the love burns still. She says it is unconditional, and I believe her.

### The Commonplace

By now we may be realising how often unconditional love has entered our life, catching us at unawares, often with joy as its companion. We find it in the company of friends; in a burst of laughter; in the 'high' of physical exhaustion, while playing a sport or running a race; in making love; in gratitude for an astonishing cloudscape, or for a glass of good wine (product of the sun and infinite care), or the grace of a bird in flight. The unconditional lover will find the Beloved's presence in the art and entertainment they enjoy: singing and sacred dance perhaps; in the TV series *The Simpsons* (recommended by Dr. Williams, Archbishop of Canterbury); in the clown Patch; in a Robin Williams' movie; in a performance of Shakespeare's *Romeo and Juliet* or *Anthony and Cleopatra*; in a Beethoven symphony, especially the *Ode to Joy*; in Tolkien's *Lord of the Rings*; in the songs of the Dixie Chicks; in countless works of classical and modern art, Filippo Lippi, Leonardo, Michelangelo, Raphael, Turner, Constable, I only mention some of the writers, artists and composers whom I particularly love. It is so easy to hold in memory one's moments of appreciation and gratitude and make them part of daily consciousness. Then it's easier to deal with the next little trouble that comes along, flat tire, missed appointment or crotchety girl or boyfriend.

Food

I have always thought it significant that Peter Caddy was fated to spend his wartime service in catering. Perhaps nowhere else, not even in medicine, could he have found a career where love is more perfectly expressed than in food preparation. Chefs love the food they produce and others share that love. The Findhorn community dining room was always packed when word got out that Peter was making omelettes. It is a truly transformative experience, making raw materials into something that nurtures the human body and soul. We should celebrate all cooks and let them know how much they are appreciated.

Lovers

Earlier, I propounded the idea that falling in love is really just Life acting out her masquerade, using Love for her own procreative purposes. Can't it be both that and love? Rarely do we experience love as unconditionally as when we are 'in love'. Many teenagers will agree and so will their distracted parents. And adults fall in love just as readily. In Rome, Cupid was depicted as blind, because lovers are blind to each other's faults. It is irrelevant that they regain their sight later, for the experience is valid *at the time*. What happens is that they see through the personality to the holy Soul within. That is Reality. The rest of the personality is Illusion.

Constancy

In the last chapter I was focusing on the difficulties that arise in marriage and committed relationships. These challenges usually derive from our personality baggage, quirks and expectations that are never apparent during the blissful 'falling in love' stage, but they may also derive from interference by relatives and, sometimes, former friends. The challenges are a test of character as well as commitment. We can choose to dismiss the concerns of the 'friends' and relatives, maintaining our relationship with them but also a certain distance, a 'no-go zone'. We can negotiate the quirks and personality habits that are causing trouble, deciding which to drop, and understanding why others are really essential. Some may be linked to one's job, like coming home sweaty and stinky from a construction site, and the necessity of having an income will be an additional factor. Even here there is likely to be some wiggle room. It would make sense to work all this out before you married, but very rarely is this done: partly because you are then in love, and the idea of marital difficulty seems a form of treason; and partly because you need to live together for a while to find out what the specific difficulties will be. This is justification for the increasingly common practice of couples living together before marriage.

There are many explanations for the high rate of divorce as compared to past times. I think it is happening because our consciousness has become increasingly individual. In former times one's identity was bound up with one's relationship. A few centuries ago a Scottish Highlander, for example, would identify himself by his relationship to his clan chief, and even in the last century a woman would see herself primarily as a wife, but now the thrust of Spirit is to have each of us identify our uniqueness. The Soul knows that our uniqueness is a facet of the Whole and seeks to ground its special quality in our personality by integrating it with every aspect of our life: relationships, work and play, all done in love. Both identification and integration are decisions that our Moral Self must take.

There is a shadow side to all things, good and bad, and the shadow side of divorce is the corresponding absence of hypocrisy in marriage: that sort of adultery mentioned in the last chapter about which the Anglican priest was complaining. All couples today face the challenge of working each one's uniqueness into the relationship; anything else is hypocrisy. If they have chosen their partner through the Spirit (and the Spirit works very unassumingly and mainly by happenstance), their two facets of uniqueness will fit well together, and may even blend to form a new uniqueness, a new facet of the Whole, while losing nothing of what was unique before.

Unconditional love is most commonly found in committed relationships and stable, tested marriage. It is often undemonstrative, sensed when we say, "I love you," and kiss when leaving for work and meeting afterwards, but it is present in every test, every project undertaken, a solid bond that is called on to resolve all challenges – sickness, wayward children, job loss, new home.

When we look around us at our friends, we will easily recognise those who love unconditionally, and that recognition forms a bond. We are attracted to them, and want to bring the same quality into our own lives. Our desire to do this speaks of the transformative power of unconditional love.

Letting Go

This story is offered me by a unique friend who is a wife and mother of grown-up children. It tells us that opportunities for unconditional love are present all the time and everywhere, choosing our vulnerable instants to reveal her lovely face. The key is to live intensely. This story tells about letting go and letting God, the same lesson that Eileen Caddy learned.

I'm not sure quite what unconditional love is, but I've certainly experienced something close to it. Not that it was me who was the giver of this love, I was the recipient.

My husband and I have been married for ten years, and I have always been pretty sure that we do really love each other. We live together, we work together, we do pretty much everything together. However there is one area of our lives that is "different," for while we have love, we do not have passion in our relationship.

Some months ago I thought I had found this passion in my life, and was utterly taken over by it. I got to know a man in an Internet bridge room; he seemed such an exciting and interesting person. He even seemed to be on the same spiritual path and have the same values as I do. I fell in love, and wanted to explore the relationship by going to meet him. My husband and I live in France; this man lived in England. I had never met him in person, and believed all he had told me.

My husband and I are committed to truth and honesty in our relationship, and I immediately shared everything with him. I suppose that even this is a part of our unconditional love for each other, that we share the difficult things openly together; we don't need to keep secrets and hide our feelings. I find great strength and freedom in being able to do this.

When I told my husband that I was in love and wanted to go and meet this man, he was devastated. I assured him that I was not going for ever, that I would be back, but that I had to explore this relationship, these strong feelings I had. I also had to admit that this could perhaps lead to a more permanent relationship but basically I believed that I was going away to have an adventure, perhaps an affair, and I still wanted my husband in my life.

It was obvious to me that my husband was extremely upset and scared; perhaps it was foolish of me to have expected it to be otherwise. I tried to put myself in his position, to imagine how I would feel. At the beginning of our relationship, 12 years ago, we had spoken of the possibility of something like this happening, for either of us, but perhaps after 12 very loving years together it had not seemed to be very likely any more. But here we were, having to face this huge challenge in our lives.

With tears in his eyes and his heart full of pain, my husband went to his computer. "I'll book your flight for you," he said. "When do you want to go?" He knew I would have problems with booking my flight in French, so he helped me do it. Next he made sure that I had all my credit cards and enough money to keep me going when I was in England. Finally, he gave me his portable phone and asked me to call him when I got there, so he could be sure I was safe.

That last evening together we went out for dinner, had a bottle of wine and talked deeply. We both spoke lovingly and caringly to each other, did everything we could to support each other through this crisis. I felt no judgement from him, no anger, just love and fear for my safety and well being.

The following morning, my husband carried my suitcase down to the station. There is a steep hill to walk down, and he did not want me to have to carry this heavy case down there. The train arrived and he kissed me goodbye. I know now that as the train left the station, he collapsed in tears and pain. But first he had made sure I was safely away, had everything I needed, and that he had done everything to make sure he had done what he could to support me.

Half an hour later my train stopped at the station where I had to change trains; I had an hour to wait for my connection. I sat on the platform, the cold wind numbing my body and mind. I sat there and began to think. I let myself compare these two men in my life. My husband who loved me so much he would let me go. And my lover who did everything to persuade me to come to him, with no thought of what that might do to my husband or me. One man who gave me everything, and the other who wanted to take it all. One man I could trust with my life, the other who was devious and encouraged me to cheat and lie.

An hour later I bought my return ticket and got on the first train back home. I suddenly remembered the portable phone and called my husband. "I'm on my way back," I told him. "I'll pick you up at the station," he replied. He gave me a big hug as I got off the train, and we made our way back up the steep hill, with him carrying my case again. Home had never looked so friendly and welcoming before. "Shall we have a cup of tea?" my husband asked. "Yes please," I replied, "and then let's talk."

And talk we did, both sharing our feelings, our fears, our needs. More than anything, we knew we loved each other. We have no guarantees that this could not happen again – for either of us. Nothing has changed dramatically in our lives. We both know that what we have is very precious, but that perhaps a day may come when we also need something else, something more. Perhaps that is what unconditional love is all about; loving without ties, without guarantees, allowing ourselves freedom to explore and grow. To look pain and confusion in the eye and still continue loving. To love in spite of fear, to welcome change, to be in each precious moment without trying to grasp it and hold it tight. Love connects and love lets go, and in letting go we come to some inkling of what unconditional love really is.

## Loyalty in Grief – Abnegation

I will follow my friend's story with that of another friend, who did not let go. N. was a Parisienne, elegant, aristocratic and kind, my mother's lifelong friend. Eighty years earlier during World War One, her husband had been a captain in the French Army and one of the hundreds of thousands who had died in the horror of Verdun. Before he left for the front, he had asked her not to remarry if he were killed. Whatever we may think of the propriety of such a request, she honoured it, refusing all offers, and there were several. At the age of 110 she died a childless widow. In all the time I spent with her, I never heard a word of self-pity. She would have been familiar with Alfred de Vigny's poem *La Mort du Loup* that tells of the hunted wolf that suffers and dies without uttering a sound ("souffre et meurt sans parler"). The poet calls this abnegation, which I see as a form of unconditional love. N. embodied it.

Saints and Angels

Many people have close relations with their Guardian Angel. Religious persons, especially Roman Catholics, often have a strong attachment to a particular saint. Communication is frequent and may be initiated from either side. Unconditional love links us to the spirit world, for it connects directly to our intuition. Do we ask who is talking to us? Yes. We must ensure that they are of the Light. For that purpose, Judy Hall's book *The Art of Psychic Protection* is invaluable.

For me, and for many Findhorn people, God is the Beloved. Our needs are known before we are aware of them, and becoming aware, we find them met. Is this the work of the Higher Self or Guardian Angel or some Higher Being? To my mind, they are all One in Spirit and any distinctions are usually a matter for them, not for me. I except the *devas* of plant species, and the elementals of individual trees and environments, both of which have a particular focus; also my Name Saint Anthony who takes an especial joy in finding things I lose – which I do rather often. What inspires me most is their constancy. It does not matter that I have been neglectful, self-absorbed or out-of-sorts. As soon as I turn to them, they are there, no recriminations, just joyful to be with me. As Krishnamurti said, we are born again in every instant.

Just Friends

The beauty of friendship is that possessive thoughts of sex and marriage do not intrude. In these circumstances it is easier to feel unconditional love. I am reminded of the biblical story of David and Jonathan, and David's song of mourning after Jonathan and his father Saul had died in battle:

> The beauty of Israel is slain upon thy high places; how are the mighty fallen!

Tell it not in Gath, publish it not in the streets of Ascalon; lest the daughters of the Philistines rejoice, lest the daughters of the uncircumcised triumph.

Ye mountains of Gilboa, let there be no dew, neither let there be rain upon you, nor fields of offerings: for there the shield of the mighty is vilely cast away, the shield of Saul, as though he had not been anointed with oil.

From the blood of the slain, from the fat of the mighty, the bow of Jonathan turned not back, and the sword of Saul returned not empty.

Saul and Jonathan were lovely and pleasant in their lives, and in their death they were not divided: they were swifter than eagles, they were stronger than lions.

Ye daughters of Israel, weep over Saul, who clothed you in scarlet and other delights, who put on ornaments of gold upon your apparel.

How are the mighty fallen in the midst of the battle! O Jonathan thou wast slain in thy high places.

I am distressed for thee, my brother Jonathan: very pleasant hast thou been unto me: thy love to me was wonderful, passing the love of women.

How are the mighty fallen and the weapons of war perished!

The beauty of the language and the razor sharpness of the imagery speak to me of the depth of David's love and keenness of his sorrow. We should not be offended by the images of violence. They are part of an old consciousness, relevant to its time but not to ours.

Love of the Natural World

Our bodies are composed of the mineral earth and it is factually correct to assert that love of the earth is in our very bones. That love expresses itself unconditionally in art: in music, as in Beethoven's *Pastoral Symphony*; in painting where the landscapes of Rembrandt and Constable, the gardens of Monet and Matisse, evoke in us the very soul of earth; and in poetry. Shelley's *Ode to a Skylark* begins, "Hail to thee, blithe spirit," and Wordsworth could write:

"My heart leaps up when I behold
A rainbow in the sky.

So may it be when I am old
Or let me die."

This is the quality of true art, that the Soul influence perceived by the artist is transmitted to the viewer. The poets of the Romantic Movement saw nature as the Nurturing Mother, but this view faded in the later literary mainstream, and Tennyson, influenced by Darwin, could write that "Nature, red in tooth and claw, ravines against the creed." Still, *The Country Diary of an Edwardian Lady* by Edith Holden is evidence that some people were still sensitive to the old consciousness that reverenced nature. First published in 1906 and republished in 1977, its sweet watercolours of birds, beasts and plants are very evocative of the beauty that inspires awe. I grew up in the same Warwickshire countryside where she had lived, and much of what she saw was still there when I was a child. Robert Louis Stevenson writes that "a little amateur painting in watercolour shows the innocent and quiet mind."

I have indicated that all material objects are the outward and visible manifestation of an indwelling spiritual principle or presence. Marko Pogacnik has recounted several of his encounters with the spirit of earth, and described her threefold presence, sometimes sweet like a bride, sometimes motherly, and sometimes terrifying, offering death; but he finds that even death is merely an opportunity for us to transform ourselves. In spiritual lore, the Blessed Virgin Mary is identified with the spirit of earth, as is St. Sophia, and I believe that the Son of Man also resides here. We may view these Beings as the redeemed spirit of earth, one that is reunited with the heavens, but there is also a more ancient version, one sickened by the evils of humankind, whose priestesses sacrificed the sacred kings, their consorts. This is the Mother Goddess of the Aegean religions, who was also the secret deity of Rome. Early Christianity saw her as its chief opponent, far more threatening than the Caesars. It was for fear of her influence that they kept out of the New Testament any reference to the formative role of women among Jesus' disciples.

The Goddess persists into the present day as the muse of artists and poets. In this aspect she is wayward, wanton, treacherous and cruel, perpetually creating and destroying. Yet her devotees can get their inspiration from no other source, and they give her unconditional love – which of course she does not return – for the joy they have in creating. Robert Graves, the late Poet Laureate, addresses her directly in his book *The White Goddess*, and her influence can be plainly read in Goethe's early poems, which are among his best. Graves describes her terrifying steed as the Night Mare, which also appears in Henry Fuseli's painting of the same name, and can be seen with snapping jaws in the White Horse which Belgic tribesmen carved in the chalk of England's Berkshire Downs centuries before the Caesars came. I believe the Goddess must have guided the movie, *The Shining*, in which Jack Nicholson starred, and also *Jaws*, as well as some of the better modern horror movies (which I refuse to watch). Yes, the Goddess is certainly still around and so are those who give her unconditional love – a true romantic love, because it is hopeless.

In recent years Wiccans have revived their ancient craft. Their reverence was always for the Sacred Mother in whose Name their forebears studied herbs and gave healing brews to sick villagers. They know her as the Great Goddess and Nurturing Mother and give her unconditional love. They refuse allegiance to the Church which persecuted their foremothers, but I sense that on the inner planes their present devotion is directed to those same Beings that I have mentioned: St. Sophia and the Blessed Virgin, Daughter of Gaia, whose renewed and inspiring presence has revived their craft.

### Animals

For many of us, animals are the perfect channels for unconditional love, both as givers and receivers. When my sweet puppy Sophie first bounded onto my lap, I felt my heart open to her, and it has not closed in the two years since. And she gives her love even more fully and spontaneously than I do. I think that spontaneity is one of the main lessons that animals can teach us. Anne Worthington, my niece and mother of four, has this to say:

> To love unconditionally, as I see it, is to love without thought of return or

thought of what is in it for you. Unconditional love is not dependent on what you get back, it is a love that knows no bounds, sets no limits or conditions and is a love that is freely given. If we love unconditionally, then our love does not change because someone behaves in a way that we don't like, it is a love that loves in spite of, or even because of, a person's behaviour.

God's love is a love that is unconditional – he will not condemn us because we make mistakes, rather he will look on us as little children, who, when they fall over, he picks up, pats on the back and sends on their way again.

I have been thinking about the behaviour of animals and the examples they set us in unconditional love. An animal loves its owner with a devotion that is unsurpassed. It doesn't matter how the owner looks, smells or behaves, the animal will just love who they are, the inner person. Can we love like that? Can we look at a tramp, with his dog by his side, and see beyond the exterior physical being and reach the perfect spiritual being within that is God, just as his dog does? If we could, I am sure that we would begin to love in a God-like way – unconditionally.

I have an old dog who is fifteen and half, and looking at her I realise that her greatest pleasure in life is to be with me. It doesn't matter if I get angry with her or shout at her or even ignore her, her love is steady and she will always be ready to be at my side.

In his book *The Daughter of Gaia* Marko Pogacnik tells us how animal souls tend to be group souls, associated with the species or with a particular flock or herd. About 20,000 years ago, certain species volunteered to associate with humans in order to learn to evolve their own individual souls. Our ignorance, particularly of that fractal of our own soul that is linked to animals, has subjected them to the miserable conditions of factory farming and total exploitation and slavery. By allowing ourselves to benefit from any part of this, as by buying some parts of the flesh that has suffered so, we compromise not only our animal friends but ourselves. By contrast, Islam insists that an animal that is to be used for food must meet a clean death at the hands of one who is ritually pure.

Machines

Eternity is longer than we think and its possibilities endlessly bizarre. If it's true, as I said of the Elohim, that Creators are responsible for their creation, what about all those machines we have been making? But they're just lifeless lumps, you will object. Wrong! I was a total unbeliever, but then I became maintenance focaliser at the Park in Findhorn and encountered too much strangeness to continue in my disbelief. I developed the concept of a hierarchy of elemental consciousness among machines, the more complex, the more evolved. Some retained the qualities of those who had made them. You usually became aware of this when you encountered a 'rogue' unit, perhaps assembled by a worker who had been in a particularly bad temper. I never tried exorcism. Perhaps I should have.

It's one of Findhorn's little jokes that you get given tasks you're quite unfitted for, and probably have been avoiding all your life; it just happens to be the job that's open when you go looking for one. For me, maintenance was one example of this humorous tendency (this book may be another). I remember an electric cooking stove that gave perpetual trouble. The electricians had done all they could, and still it failed. I knew nothing about electricity except that it was dangerous (I'd put my finger in a light socket – that's 230 volts in England – when I was four), but I knew I had to examine the stove myself. The problem was so simple. The stove was just incredibly dirty! In my perception, it was very unhappy. Focused on their skills, the electricians had ignored the dirt. I might not know much about maintenance but I knew how to clean, and that's what I did, top to bottom, inside and out. When I had finished, I swear I heard purring. I issued some stern injunctions about regular weekly cleaning and heard no more.

More challenging still was the idea that machinery and fittings might take on the qualities of their owners. I remember being called to a caravan that was about ten or fifteen yards away from the house where Eileen Caddy was living. The caravan door was of metal and gave an electric shock to whoever touched it: not dangerous, but enough to cause a tingle even in dry weather. Eventually, I don't remember how, I traced the problem to a shorted light fitting in Eileen's sitting room. I told her, "When an ordinary person has an electrical problem, they just fuse their own fittings, but you electrify the neighbourhood!" She was rather pleased.

The author Arthur C. Clarke has said that while not all science fiction is true prophecy, all true prophecy is contained in science fiction. This makes me think of all the novels about machines becoming conscious. Usually they are horror stories; the machines realise they can think faster and more logically than fallible humans, and decide to take over the world. That's certainly as likely a scenario as their reverencing us as their Creator God. So the question becomes, how do you impart conscience to a machine? Actually, they acquire it from you. There's a troubling thought! The problems that faced my God after Day Seven seem nothing compared to the problems that will face us if we are held responsible for our machines. Is this how we shall be tested as a human race, to give unconditional love to our creation? Though it may not be so difficult. Men (why is it usually men?) do tend to have love affairs with their machines, particularly cars, and not always because they're the latest, fastest, sexiest model around. There's an American TV advertisement that runs, "You're born, you die, and in between, if you're lucky, you get to work on cars." Yes, eternity may be longer than we think! Am I kidding? I really don't know, and that's part of the wonder and joy of being human.

*Exercise*

*Think of an instance when you have given or received unconditional love. Take the memory with you into the Silence. Let it fill your Soul.*

## *PART THREE*

# SOCIETY

The Lord careth for the strangers;
he defendeth the fatherless and widow:
as for the way of the ungodly,
he turneth it upside down.

*[Book of Common Prayer]*

How long, O Lord, how long?

*[Thomas Babington Macaulay]*

# 12. Living Consciously

"See that you have an aim, a goal in life."

*[Eileen Caddy]*

People who have made Spirit the basis for their lives will know that, for this lifetime, they have chosen a path: for those inclined towards activism it may be the Path of the Warrior; for others, the Path of the Contemplative; the Path of the Householder; or another path. They are all ways to express our love of God. Those following the Path of the Householder may be unaware that they are following a spiritual path; just that they are coping with the bills, ensuring there is a roof to live under, getting the children to school and seeing there is food on the table. They should know that the Archangel Michael says that this Path offers us an unparalleled learning experience about the nature of Spirit. Nonetheless, people following this path often feel stuck, and that makes loving difficult.

There is another version of the Path, one just as important as the Paths mentioned above. It concerns your spiritual themes in this lifetime, the qualities you are to embody in yourself. These themes are not simplistic, but will vary for each man and woman. When we know what they are, we can be on the look out to practice them in all we do. I call this 'living consciously'. In meditation, we should ask what qualities we are to embody in this lifetime, and wait for an answer. I think it is important to eliminate words or thoughts of 'trying' from the question. To 'try' is a recipe for failure, because anyone can try, and the 'trying' in itself becomes success. So go for the gold, and ask for the qualities you are to embody, not trying to embody. We are here to spiritualise matter and our least success in bringing a spiritual quality into our incarnate being is a step in the right direction.

*Exercise*

*In meditation, ask what are your life's guiding themes. Wait for an answer. Do not worry if this takes its time – days, months or years. It will come when you are ready. When you receive it, consider how well your present activities fit your life themes. Consider what you might adjust for greater consistency and happiness. Write down your thoughts in your journal.*

The answers may come only after a lapse of time, in some unguarded moment like awakening from sleep, and they may surprise you. If they are truthful, you will not be able to forget them, even years later. When you know them, it pays to be mindful how each encounter can enlarge your understanding how to apply them. The Archangel Michael, in another of his messages to Ana Pogacnik, has said that nothing happens in our lives that is meaningless, not even the least interaction with another. There are no chance encounters. We should pay attention to everyone and everything we meet, to discover what we may learn, and in learning, give. It may help to write down your insights in a journal.

I do not remember how my experience of my own life themes originated, whether I asked for it or whether it came spontaneously. I rather think the latter because it was accompanied by the sweetest angelic intimations, a sense of peace and joy and more than that, of caring, that filled my soul and touched my etheric body with gentle caresses. The themes came to me as feelings: empathy, compassion, joy; and on a different plane, perseverance, endurance, courage and love. I recognise these as having been leading elements in my life, even before I knew of them consciously. When I work with the physically and mentally challenged, they require the exercise of all the above qualities, and in return they offer unconditional love.

I hesitated before sharing my experience with you, in case the example of my themes might distract you from your own truth. Yours will be individual to you, and mine are not a model. The important thing is for you to identify your own life themes, and learn to apply them in your career and in each 'chance' encounter. That will assure you that you are living your life on the right moral path, which is a recipe for happiness. Then it becomes natural to give and receive love, unconditional or appropriate as circumstances indicate.

*Exercise*

*Take a quiet moment to think about your current relationships; then select one and ask which of your themes does it demand of you, and which do you receive from it. How can you make your practice of the theme more conscious and intense? When you have finished exploring that relationship, go on to another, and another, for as long as you can sustain the energy. For some acquaintances and relatives the need to love and forgive will be paramount, but each one will also have individual, special gifts to offer and receive. Write down your insights.*

---

# 13. THE WORLD TURNED UPSIDE DOWN

The battle goes sore against us to the going down of the sun.
*Robert Louis Stevenson*

Systemic Problems and Solutions

In the 1960s Katherine Whitehorn wrote a humorous article in the London *Observer*, suggesting that our Western society is based on the medieval Church's seven deadly sins – pride, greed, lust, jealousy, envy and sloth. She excepted gluttony, which was not fashionable in England at the time, but has now become *cause celebre* in the USA, where 30 percent of the population are accounted obese. This fits with something I remember reading, that what humanity calls progress is, in the angelic view, regress from day one. The angels have a point if we are to see progress as increasing awareness of God and the ability to co-create. Our material achievements have been great, but face it, we have made something of a hell here on earth. All despite our best intentions. We offer welfare programs to ease poverty, but find they must be made conditional in order to prevent the recipients falling into the slump of dependency. Visitors to poor villages in Asia and Africa marvel that the people there can be so happy, despite having little more than basic necessities. I think it's because they live for the day and take each moment as it comes. If your cooking stove is a few pieces of charcoal laid on the ground, you don't have to worry about your stock portfolio.

Of course, poverty is not the only problem or even the worst. There's pollution, global warming, over-population, disease, starvation, terror, each feeding into one another and compounded by regional wars over religion, territory and race. The problems are systemic and the currently proposed systemic solution is the globalisation of capitalism. The poorer countries are suspicious that this will be a tool for their further exploitation, becoming labelled as quaint tourist destinations and low-wage producers for multinational corporations. The standard response is that global capitalism will generate the necessary wealth to fund specific initiatives directed to their individual problems.

Here we confront a very ugly, never admitted problem. Despite the successes of capitalism, its nature ensures that it will never offer a more than partial solution to economic problems, though it can provide useful palliatives. Its deficiency is inherent in its pricing structure that puts a value on scarcity. The scarcity may be real like crop failures, or contrived like the supply of oil. Displayed mathematically, Scarcity=Profit. The result is always profit and power for the haves, and loss and lack, ranging from inconvenience to starvation, for the have-nots. Communism and Socialism tried to offer alternatives, and both came unstuck. These were top-down initiatives directed by the state. Bottom-up initiatives, responding to local needs but thinking globally and altruistically, may be more successful. Such endeavours can take very diverse forms, matching available skills and facilities with needs. Such a movement is already happening. For example, a web of privately owned enterprises working under a co-operative umbrella is currently evolving in the Findhorn Community.

To overcome the Scarcity=Profit syndrome, we need to change our laws and concepts to enable resources that are owned in common to be used for the common good. I am thinking primarily of solar energy, which has not been widely exploited because, as the saying goes, 'no one owns the sun'. Oil energy is an example of how scarcity is created for private profit. Because we operate in a closed economic system – the planet – no one is actually robbed thereby, because the profits go back into the system. However, the system itself is constricted. Everyone is poorer as a result, but the ones least affected are those who already have the most. Energy is such a basic resource that its costs enter into everyone's budget, not just of consumers but producers too. Its cost and scarcity adversely affect enterprises at every level. At the moment, the only energy sources in wide use are those that pollute the most: coal, oil and nuclear. If solar and wind energy were more widely used, their cost would come down. Then more energy would be available locally, and it would be non-polluting.

What does this have to do with unconditional love? I think that our outside reflects our inside, and that as we come to terms with unconditional love and begin to practice it in any of its myriad varieties, we shall see the world change around us. The key lies in ourselves, and the changes will reflect who we are and who we are becoming. I believe the external changes will be towards an organically organised economy, reflecting what humanity truly is: Body, Soul and Spirit. Such an outcome is difficult to conceptualise and I suggest that it's important not to do so. I remember Peter Caddy telling how, in the early days at Findhorn, he had a pile of crazy paving (irregular shapes and assorted sizes of limestone slabs) delivered to make pathways around the cedar wood bungalows that had just been installed. For him, work was love in action and he went ahead, following his intuition, never thinking about the layout, and when he had finished everyone told him how original and perfect the pathways were. I also remember my friend George Ripley, architect of Findhorn's Universal Hall, telling me how, when it was nearly finished, people would come to him, saying things like, "What a wonderful idea to make the ratio of those two spaces equal to the ratio of the moon's size to that of earth." He didn't know that they were, and had certainly never thought about it.

The Hall was built with unconditional love – I was there and saw how the builders related to the concept and their part in it. They worked hard but were relaxed and joyful, coming up with ideas that were discussed and evaluated over tea breaks, along with whatever else was going on in their lives. The teams built a group consciousness focused around a heart commitment that encouraged each person to show their human side without fear of judgement. Nothing was omitted on the practical side – all proper plans were drawn up and permits obtained – but a heart dimension was added. Mistakes were sometimes made, for the concept was continually evolving, but in my opinion they were fewer than in regular building projects, and none were disastrous. Findhorn is worth a visit just to attend a performance at the Universal Hall. It is a building that inspires and draws people within.

My point is that if you try to plan what the new age will be like, you interfere with its natural unfolding. This concept must be the hardest thing for our intellectual age to come to terms with – that things can go well when you don't think too deeply about them. That doesn't speak to a careless attitude. It requires commitment of another sort: to acknowledge that what is best for the whole must be best for you too; then to go into meditation and ask what, in practical terms, is best for you and how to go about manifesting it, one step at a time. If you see things around you changing in a natural, organic way, you'll know that you are on the right track, in tune with the universe. Think about the High Street of an English town that has evolved naturally over the centuries, without centralised planning. Ignore the modern shop fronts and chain stores; see it as it was for a few brief decades before bad taste prevailed. The scene is varied, appropriate and beautiful. There was a guiding spirit there, and it was the Angel of the town, its astral Soul, made up of the interlaced consciousness of every individual inhabitant, a whole evolving into Wholeness. If we ask the Angels of our different communities to guide and inspire us, the body and soul of the new age will evolve appropriately. Angels are One in Spirit and co-operation will replace conflict.

I do not wish to demean the intellectual side of our human nature. The intellect we have evolved is a great gift, but it has identified itself with

Mephisto, and when we use it alone we are like a person hobbling on one leg along a perilous path. When we develop a heart consciousness for sake of balance, we walk on two legs and know to direct our steps into more wholesome ways. If you don't believe that the heart has a consciousness, I recommend that you read *The Heart's Code* by Paul Pearsall. He tells how two doctors became intrigued by accounts of heart transplant patients who remembered incidents from the donors' lives. They researched the data and found there was a pattern that suggested that memory, at least, is independent of the brain. One person had received a murder victim's heart. The case was unsolved, but the recipient was able to provide the police with such details that the perpetrator was identified, and with other evidence then brought to light, convicted.

*Exercise*

*Go within and let your consciousness drift towards your heart. What do you feel? Sensations of warmth perhaps? Peace? Stay there as long as you want or can. Then give thanks and carry the feelings with you into your daily life. Practise this as often as you like.*

I would go so far as to propose that no blueprint conceived out of pure intellect will ever come up with an ideal solution to the world's problems – or even approach close. On the other hand, an organically grown, co-operatively based economy, giving scope to human enterprise and free will but outlawing exploitation of living beings and the degradation of the environment, instead encouraging the use of resources held in common – that will come close. We have the option of creating the legal forms to promote it while we still have an enforcement structure to prevent criminal disruption such as has occurred in South Africa and Russia, or we can continue to tinker with our present system. If we follow our present course and the world's problems get out of hand and breakdown occurs, then the outcome will be very problematical. So we need to take appropriate action early, on the outer and on the inner, while focusing on the positive: Practice unconditional love and let the inner be reflected in the outer; Hold the vision of your goal; Let go and let

God; Take whatever positive action in the concrete world that is suggested to you and lies ready to your hand.

*Manifestation Exercise*

*In the exercise at the end of Chapter Ten, you asked yourself what you had left undone that you would still like to do. Go back to that idea and follow these steps:*

*1. If you now know your life themes as suggested in the previous chapter on 'Living Consciously', consider how your idea relates to them. If positively, consider the upside and downside. Is it something you want unconditionally? If not, build the conditions into your agenda.*

*2. Go within. Ask if this idea of yours is really in accordance with the divine plan and good for the whole. If the answer is no, release it and ask what you should focus on instead.*

*3. When you are answered positively, build an image of the idea's achievement. How will it look? How will it feel? Add details, touch, sound, smell. A calendar showing the date is a good idea, since you are tapping into the eternal consciousness that doesn't have an exact idea of time.*

*4. When you have the details of your image ready, make them as precise as possible. Fill them with glowing colour. Make them beautiful.*

*5. Now let yourself really want your image to manifest in the concrete world. Fill yourself with desire for it. Fill yourself till you feel you're bursting!*

*6. At a certain point there will be something like a click inside your mind. This means that the image has descended from the astral realms of the emotion to the etheric plane, and is now ready to descend to the physical. Release the image now and give most humble and hearty thanks that it has already happened. This is the final step, your firm belief that manifestation has already occurred. Be sure that it will descend to the physical world at the appropriate time.*

*7. Continue your life with the thought that your idea is real and has already manifested. Be grateful that it is already with you and blessing you. Gratitude is key, the more intense the better. Do not worry about your idea or even think of it, except to be grateful. Do not write about it in your journal, because that would be an inappropriate manifestation.*

Pain and Suffering

It is unfortunate the Church's teaching of God's omnipotence has led its followers to believe that all the ills befalling them are his will, whereas usually they arise from their own karma. Some nonetheless continue in humble faith, but some find the pain too much and fall away from belief. It does take a leap of faith to accept that some terrible event is really a learning experience on the road to Spirit. It takes commitment to cultivate the detachment that recognises pain and pleasure as equally illusory, diversions from the true path, as *A Course in Miracles* tells us. In her book *Kitchen Table Wisdom*, Dr. Remen tells how cancer sufferers can feel a sense of release and freedom, and be suffused with joy. We need discernment to distinguish pleasure from joy, whose presence in a person, teachers say, is an unfailing indication of God's indwelling. Is the distinction nit-picking? Not really. Pleasure comes from outside of us, joy from inside, but there is no reason why both can't exist together.

Spiritual lore says that pain teaches us love. In the nineteenth century doctors and husbands used this to excuse the pains of childbirth, for then all doctors were men and painkillers little used. Modern thinking regards this as a merely male excuse for lack of awareness, and today not many women refuse painkillers when giving birth. However, that is what a friend of mine did. She relates that she prepared for natural childbirth in hospital, refused all sedation before, during and after the event, and was totally connected throughout. The pain she experienced, and it was not light, was totally subsumed in the unconditional love which engulfed her.

Being a man, and one with considerable aversion to pain, I am very tentative about advancing this hypothesis about pain in childbirth. However, that is the story of one woman I know well, and I have heard of others. In the last section of book, I suggest that Jesus used the pain of crucifixion and his unconditional love for humankind as vehicles for his resurrection.

Patriotism and Love of Country

In my parish church in England, the memorial chapel to the dead of two world wars is inscribed with Jesus' words, "Greater love has no man than this, that he lays down his life for his friends." As I experienced my young patriotism during World War Two when we were threatened with invasion, it was not so much for my friends that I was going to use my small shotgun and lay down my life, rather a strong feeling that the only appropriate place for German paratroopers on English earth was beneath it. My family must have shared my conviction. Though none of us spoke of our plans till long afterwards, each of us had selected a weapon and chosen where we would lie in wait. Had not Churchill said, "You can always take one with you." At the height of the war, an 'old boy' returned to preach in my school chapel. He was the Right Reverend Winnington Ingram, Bishop of London, third ranked prelate of the Church of England. He was over eighty and looked frail but his voice thundered as he told us, "Do not confuse service to your country with service to God."

In the U.S. military today, service to God and country are synonymous. Winnington Ingram would have called this blasphemy, and I think he would be right. In Jesus' words, it is the distinction between giving to God and giving to Caesar. They may run together, as I think they did in some aspects of World War Two, but they should never be conjoined. Patriotism involves killing or training to kill, and that is the problem. Or is it? In the *Bhagavad Gita*, Sri Krishna tells the wavering Arjuna, "He who sees himself as slayer or who thinks of himself as slain, both understand not; he slays not, nor is slain. He is never born nor dies…" He concludes that Arjuna must go forth and fight. "Either slain, thou wilt gain heaven or, conquering, thou wilt enjoy the earth;" The *Gita* was written 5,000 years ago and though its words still ring true, I think that, as our Soul has evolved, so have the learning experiences required of us. St. Francis of Assisi suggests a different course. He lived in the time of the Crusades and his solution, recounted in James Twyman's book *Portrait of the Master*, was to go to the enemy, not to fight him but to convert him, and make peace. He failed, as did Rudolf Hess in World War Two, but *A Course in Miracles* tells us that what we count as our greatest failures may be our greatest successes – and vice-versa.

Duty

Whether or not we approve of armies, military service offers unparalleled opportunities to manifest unconditional love. Of course, this is a by-product, not the intention – one of God's little ironies. On countless occasions men and women have risked their lives to drag a wounded comrade out of the line of fire. It happens even in peacetime. I remember reading of the Regimental Sergeant-Major who was training recruits on the use of live grenades. The training site was a trench for protection from exploding fragments, and a high bank in front of it was thought to be an additional safeguard. The soldiers were lined up in the trench and each man in turn must throw a grenade over the bank. A nervous soldier did not throw hard enough and the grenade rolled back. As it fell into the trench, the Sergeant-Major threw himself upon it and died when it exploded half a second later.

---

## 14. ROCKS IN THE RAPIDS

Never try to interfere with anyone else's path.

*[Eileen Caddy]*

I have the faith that unconditional love is the underlying current of the earth – what gave it birth and sustains its life and motion. As I look around me, I see its strength increasing as more and more people, even corporations, relate to the sense of community, which is a sort of loving. Soon it will be irresistible.

When we give ourselves up to love, it will bear us gently where we need to go, which is where we most want to be. I have been accused of being Pollyanna, and that's okay. My answer is, the process works. But I don't deny there are some troubling impediments to love's flow, built into our society's institutions. It's counterproductive to fight them – that merely builds their energy – but we can consider how to avoid and change them. Can we do that by extending unconditional love to the persons involved, rather than the institutions they represent? For instance, there are many priests of outstanding integrity and compassion, whose institutions still hang onto notions of exclusivity and elitism. Let's have a look at two important classes of institutions.

Corporations

Corrupt corporations have been in the news lately, those making billions for insiders but depriving employees of their pensions and stockholders of their investments. Love cannot focus on the evil that they did but must look for the good qualities they possess. Those CEOs were very capable people, but dazzled by wealth and power. They acted as if they were gods. The practical Romans were aware of this human failing, and when they honoured a victorious general with a triumphal procession, they had a slave stand beside him in his chariot to whisper in his ear, amid the plaudits of the crowd, "Remember thou art mortal." The root of the problem is the culture that the institutions engender, one where the focus is misplaced. In corporations the focus is on the bottom line, and then all values fall to the bottom.

The Churches

Ossification seems to overwhelm any long-lived institution. It demands loyalty, sometimes at the expense of the ideals it was founded to serve. Unconditional love can only be given and received by living beings. Even our landscapes and Earth herself are alive by virtue of their indwelling spirits, but if the life has died, as has happened in many human institutions, love can be neither given nor received. The Church is no exception. God seems to want us to live intensely, be entirely committed, witness the letter to the Church of the Laodiceans in Revelations, "I know thy works, that thou art neither cold nor hot: I would thou wert cold or hot." But many Churches approve moderate behaviour, following the lead of government.

The Social Scene

Society has always been split between the conventional and wilder spirits, and we have no way of measuring whether the gap is wider now than yesteryear. On the one hand, our culture is suffused by sex, violence and addiction. Some adults seek palliatives in affairs, gambling, cheating, swinging, prostitution and the pursuit of money; others, more passively, watch soaps that portray hatred, competition and unscrupulousness. Much teen culture dismisses spirituality and engages instead in rap music that exalts violence.

That's one side of the story. On the other side are those who flee to the refuge of religion, but in Europe they are few. In the USA, religion is often fundamentalist and elitist, looking for the Rapture when the chosen few will be taken up to heaven. *A Course in Miracles* asks if one could be happy in heaven if a fellow human remained in hell. The fundamentalists find as much inspiration in the Old Testament, with its violence and doctrine of the Chosen People, as in the New. In his book *Indaba My Children*, Credo Mutwa, keeper of the sacred history of the Zulu nation, recounts a legendary incident where the Guardian Goddess of one age of consciousness appears in the next as a Demon bent on destruction. Makes sense. When we evolve, the old values no longer hold. This is the terrible flaw in what is known as Judaic Christianity, very prevalent in the USA and a contradiction in terms. Translated into today's world of Middle Eastern strife, it is especially dangerous. Clearly referring to the Old Testament, St. Paul writes, "The letter kills, but the spirit gives life," also that "all things are become new." Divine qualities do not change, but our capacity to understand and interpret them does. The Father of the New Testament is not the Yahweh of the Old. The Old Testament is best read as the story of a people's emerging consciousness of God. This assessment is in no way intended to denigrate the spirit of Judaism, whose inspired traditions and commentaries contain so much warm and heart-filled material.

Between the two extremes, Lucifer and Satan, are those who follow the Christ path, living modestly perhaps, always keeping faith with themselves. They are everywhere, teenagers and adults, in every walk and condition of life, for they are aspects of God's multi-dimensionality. They do not push their beliefs, but you will recognise them by the joy in their eyes. They are the leaven of hope.

Fear of God

If St. John's words are true, that perfect love casts out fear, the contrary should also hold good: that fear casts out love. Take a look around and see how fear plays into our daily lives. Much of advertising relies on it. For every message of hope there are two of fear: fear of being sick; of being second best; of not having the most fashionable clothes or glamorous home. That's a lesson we all must learn early on the path to unconditional love, not to fear what people think, and to carefully research the truth of what we are told.

If you were brought up in the Christian religion, you were probably told when quite young that "fear of the Lord is the beginning of wisdom." But if you have followed a spiritual path, you will soon have begun to ask, "Why should I fear my Beloved?" And of course, you shouldn't, rather embrace him, her or it – as the case may be – and pledge mutual and everlasting devotion. Does that sound a bit much? Believe me, when you meet, there's no alternative. But there may still be a few Biblical hang-ups to haunt you. For instance, Jesus said, "Follow me!" Does that mean to crucifixion? I used to think so, and got rather discouraged, knowing that I was not up to it. Later I learned that what was done once was done for all, and for all time. But God gives us many easier opportunities to show our love, such as volunteering to help and heal others, working among the poor or nurturing the planet's forests and wildlife. Resurrection, not crucifixion, is important. Perfect love casts out fear.

*Exercise*

*Think about your life. Do you wobble between the two extremes, even in thought? Go within and ask for guidance, how you may stay on the Christ path.*

# 15. The Communist

I have loved justice and hated iniquity:
therefore I die in exile.

*[Pope Gregory VII]*

Vernon Beranger, steadfast and sardonic, was my friend. I think he would have been amused and vaguely insulted to find himself accused of unconditional love. He was a trial attorney in South Africa, devastating in cross-examination, and very high-priced when he defended rich and guilty whites. For poverty-stricken blacks, accused of various crimes under the inequitable apartheid laws, he was a star of hope, charging nothing. He was an anomaly in race-conscious South Africa: an Afrikaner whose family had lived in the country for three hundred years; owner of a 40,000 acre 'farm' where he hunted the wild animals which made it their home; an atheist; a communist and a millionaire who defended blacks.

I was never sure how deep his communist convictions were. Black freedom was his passion. He was committed to that ideal, and often visited the communist countries which were openly hostile to apartheid and the only ones to provide funds and education to help the resistance movement. Certainly, his politics caused him great inconvenience. 'Banned' by the government, he was forbidden to attend any gathering of more than five people and so could not attend his own daughter's wedding. But they could not stop him practising law and they did not take away his passport, which he used to travel abroad and rally support. We were always told of his visits to communist countries, but he was a master of complexity, as this story demonstrates.

In 1964 he was part of the team defending Nelson Mandela against a charge of treason. The prosecution had irrefutable documentary evidence. Treason carried a mandatory death sentence and the state would have liked nothing better than to get rid of Mandela once and for all. Vernon's solution was to call in all his chips and put his career on the line. Communist countries had no official influence with the South African government, but Western countries did. In the West, criticism of apartheid was still restrained and ineffective, but many officials and politicians disliked it intensely and Vernon must have made a point of fostering connections with some important personalities. These people were aware of Mandela's charismatic appeal and could envisage him as a leader who might extricate South Africa from its predicament without civil war and bloodshed. Vernon sent a copy of Nelson Mandela's defence speech to one leading individual in Britain and another in the USA, and to two other Western countries. This speech was not so much a defence as an indictment, accusing the South African Government of instigating the crimes for which he was charged, for their laws had left blacks no recourse but illegal activity. It was an extraordinarily eloquent document and was later made into a recording.

Vernon's purpose was to give the Western governments a tool and a motive to bring diplomatic pressure on the South Africans to drop the treason charge. This would save Mandela from the death penalty. He would be sentenced to prison, but he would be alive, and then, who knew what miracles might happen? But Vernon had to give the Western governments time to make their diplomatic moves. Once the death sentence was passed, the South Africans would say that justice must take its course. His solution was to send the speech out of the country secretly, six weeks before it was due to be delivered. This was contempt of court and, if made public, Vernon could have been disbarred for life.

He chose couriers to carry the speech out. I was one. We sat in his car outside his office while he gave me instructions. The office was bugged for sound but not vision, he told me, and I should make conversation as if I was consulting him about a business matter. We went in and he opened the safe and handed me a manila envelope. We returned to his car without incident and I flew out the next day. Arriving in London, I followed instructions and, in true cloak and dagger style, stood on the steps of a Government building at a certain time, to be met by a tall stranger who knew my name. I handed him the envelope. He told me it would be put in the diplomatic bag and delivered next day to Adlai Stevenson, US Ambassador to the United Nations.

Eventually Vernon had to go into exile, where he died before the great changes that brought democracy to his country. Freedom is the air that Spirit breathes, its absolute necessity, and it's fair to say he gave his life for it, enduring great personal hardship and danger. There were others who put themselves in the same line of fire: Father Huddleston and Bishop Tutu as they then were, Chief Luthuli and Mandela himself, but they all had the Christian faith and the promise of eternal life to sustain them. Vernon had nothing but his own integrity and passionate love of freedom. To act as he did, you must reach deep into your soul and there discover the purest fire, without any thought of end gaining. This was the unconditional love of Vernon Beranger. When Nelson Mandela was released from prison to become President of a free South Africa, I can imagine his great "Halloo!" of joy ringing through the halls of Heaven.

*Exercise*

*What thoughts came to you as you read this Chapter? Surprise? Consternation? Disbelief? Or gratitude? Go into the Silence and let God's love cover you as the waters cover the sea.*

---

## 16. The Role of Evil*

O benefit of ill! Now I find true
That better is by evil still made better.

*[William Shakespeare]*

Some thirty years ago I was walking in Cluny woods near Findhorn, wondering about a friend's decision to take his wife and child abroad to follow a charismatic guru who was being touted as the New Messiah. My upbringing

* (Parts of this chapter were originally published on www.planetlightworker.com and are reprinted here by kind permission of the editor.)

had made me suspicious of all such claims and I wondered darkly whether this person was not the Anti-Christ, rather than the Crucified One. Clear as a bell into my consciousness came the message, "All is of Me." I was astounded at the temerity of such a claim. It destroyed a large part of my identity, fixated on the struggle between good and evil which I had inherited from my Anglican religion and a childhood during World War Two. Now I was being asked to believe that good and evil were two sides of the same coin.

I did not doubt the truth of the message nor its divine source. It met the test for messages purporting to be of the Light: both its arrival and its content were totally unexpected. Also, the woods had been a sacred grove for millennia. I pondered the evidence. Had not God allowed our first forebears to be tempted? In the Bible too, the devil appears before God and obtains permission to tempt Job. In an Arab legend about the creation of humanity, half the souls are foreordained to salvation, the other half to damnation, presumably because they are evil. There is a Hindu story how the King of the Demons had offended the God Vishnu, the Preserver. To restore balance in the universe, Vishnu gave him a choice, to assist him seven times, or to oppose him three.

It is a mechanical fact that without friction, there can be no progress. The image of a car is often used. If there were no friction between the tire and the road, the car would not move. We may see the road as life and the car as ourselves. The friction is what we call evil, because movement is change, and if we are honest, we much prefer to stand still, or only allow progress within a setting of stability. But, reading the fossil record, scientists have come to realize that evolution does not happen like that. It progresses by leaps, usually occasioned by some crisis in the environment. I believe this to be as true on the soul and spiritual levels as it is on the physical.

We can apply these thoughts to the recent horror of the twin towers in New York and the war on terrorism in which the world is being invited to participate. There is a body of expert opinion which holds that the larger roots of terror do not lie so much in fundamentalist religion as in the split between the haves and the have-nots, wide now and growing wider. This is as true in the United States, where for the past two decades the rich have been getting richer faster and the poorest have seen their standards decline, as it is in the rest of the world.

The developed nations seem determined to carry the process further through economic globalisation, a euphemism for 'capitalist rule'. At the Asian economic summit in October 2001, the Prime Minister of Malaysia warned U.S. President Bush that the globalisation process would drive the poor nations further into poverty. The President rejected the argument, ignoring that it is the relative poverty of two thirds of the world that fuels the terrorists' rage and enlists their recruits. As television carries messages of Western prosperity to the majority of others who are excluded, the dangers of widening terror will grow. How can the developed countries expect success in the war against terror when their policies are robbing poorer countries of their independence and self-sufficiency, fuelling the poverty that is at the root of terror?

There is always a choice. You can get involved in the struggle mindlessly, on the good side of course. Or you can realise that either side will appear good to certain mind-sets and look rather at what the struggle is going to accomplish. Then you can make a more informed choice. From this perspective, President Bush and Osama Bin Laden, Saddam Hussein or whoever is the next candidate-in-waiting, look like Tweedle Dum and Tweedle Dee, leading the Dance of Unintended Consequences which is invoked whenever war is declared. And those consequences could involve a breakdown of institutions in the Middle East, causing chaos in Europe and America. If the process goes a certain distance, we can expect a further consequence, the evolutionary leap that occurs when conditions get critical.

Are we due for such a leap? Some important Americans think so. Watts, a Reaganite Secretary of the Interior, had plans for the further degradation of the nation's forests and rangelands, which he defended by implying that we wouldn't need them for much longer. The U.S. Christian fundamentalists, an influential voting bloc, see the re-establishment of the State of Israel as evidence that the trauma and horror of the End Times are at hand, as foretold in the Book of Revelations. By fervently backing Israel, they demonstrate their willingness to assist.

Unheeded in the turmoil is Jesus' injunction, "That ye return not evil: but whosoever shall smite thee in thy right cheek, turn to him the other also." (Mat. 5:39) He also said, "He that is not with me is against me." (Mat. 12:30) This puts the smitten USA in an uncomfortable position. If these really are the End Times, then we are involved in a climactic struggle, not between good and evil – that would be no contest – but between the two forces of evil, Lucifer and Satan. The conflict may well be projected into the physical world, though this is unnecessary, for the real battle is in our hearts which are shutting out the Christ. It is when the two evils have exhausted themselves and we see their transparent folly that the Christ will arise in our hearts and minds and we will know Him for Ourself.

Einstein is said to have remarked that only two things were infinite: the universe and human stupidity; and he was not sure about the universe. Marko Pogacnik tells us that the planet is already engaged in evolutionary transformation, and the human race, a necessary component, is lagging. Since we are unwilling or unable to pay heed to what is going on, our pleasant human space must needs get upset. Evolution does not occur in the stable conditions of complacency, but requires work, willing or no. Evil provides the spur, for it forces us to see the best in everything, even in itself. By the time this book is printed we may have gone much further down a destructive road; or the nations of the world may be prevailing on the USA and Israel to undo the policies that led to terror and instead seek reconciliation, marginalizing the terrorists. Then we could open our hearts to the Christ and adapt without trauma to the evolutionary transformation that is occurring. The whole point of prophecy is to warn, so we may avoid it.

## Loving the Criminal – Forgiveness

How is it that a criminal, who has committed a most horrific crime and may even be facing death, can still confidently assert that he is saved and is with God? While working in an American Department of Corrections I have heard officials scoff at such presumption, but it is for their souls I fear, not the criminal's. The unhappy truth is that the Christ experience is a death experience. As Dr. Johnson remarked, "When a man knows he is to be hanged in a fortnight, it concentrates his mind wonderfully." The death may be psychological, when the personality dies and is reborn anew; in a way, that is choice, when you fall on the cornerstone and are broken. Or the death may be physical, as happened when I met the Son of Man, and the cornerstone fell on me and ground me to powder! Understand that I do not advocate the death penalty and dislike punishment in all its forms, preferring accountability and restitution, but experience tells us that consciousness of crime and retribution can lead to salutary changes in the personality. I remember a whale hunter saying that he had never realised that harpooning was wrong until an outlaw organisation sank his ship!

Society is tarnished when it engages in executions and lengthy prison sentences. Other approaches can achieve character changes in a more humane manner and bring greater social benefits. Sometimes confrontation will bring about a softening of attitudes, inspiring in the criminal the desire to make restitution, and in the victim an understanding of the circumstances of the crime. For my part, I believe we will never have an equitable system of justice as long as we deny the influence exerted by former lives on the interactions between criminals and victims. Often a past life victim is today's perpetrator; it simply means that they have learned nothing. Marko Pogacnik reports a communication from the Archangel Michael, saying that nothing happens that our Soul has not accepted as necessary for our learning. Of course our Moral Self has free will to reject it.

It is a terrible truth that the violent death of a family member may project their loved ones into the Christ experience. This thought came to me as I watched the Oprah Show *Incredible Stories of Forgiveness*, which first aired in the USA on April 22, 2002. The people interviewed had been brutally attacked or had witnessed the murder of a family member, and yet had come to forgive the perpetrator. Their stories may have more to do with forgiveness than unconditional love, but the two qualities are very close. I heard one woman say how the act of forgiveness had given her control over her own life, empowering her to make new friends, be a mother, do well at work, instead of being run by anger and misery over what had happened to her. One mother had lost her daughter and her own mother when another mother, drunk and speeding, had crashed into her van. She asked herself how could that other mother, with three children, be drunk at 7:30 in the morning? Out of that asking came compassion and out of that, forgiveness. She wrote her, met and offered friendship. She told Oprah that she had given what was given to her: the unconditional love of God. And out of that compassion, forgiveness and unconditional love, the once drunken mother has given up alcohol and turned her life around. These people have achieved closure. In contrast, we often hear how the punishment of a criminal brings no lasting satisfaction to the bereaved relatives, and the closer they were to the victim, the less the sense of completion.

*Exercise*

*Have you personally suffered some injury that you can't forgive? Muster your courage, go into the Silence and ask to be shown the Way.*

*PART FOUR*

# GOD

Where can I go from Your Spirit?
Where can I flee from Your Presence?
If I go up to the Heavens, You are there.
If I make my bed in the depths, You are there.

*[Psalm 139]*

# 17. THE UNCONDITIONALITY OF GOD

"Why not excel in everything you do?"

*[Eileen Caddy]*

Usually God stands beside me like a familiar friend, supportive and helpful, telling me, when I remember to ask, where I am slipping up. Occasionally I am reminded of the true gulf that separates us, and how all-round compassionate She/He is to step down across the levels and communicate in this way. I remember a time when my partner was in Inverness Hospital awaiting the birth of our child, and I was working with a group at Cluny. Like all fathers I was worried about the outcome of the birth, and I asked the group to meditate with me and ask for a safe and happy delivery. I was vouchsafed no answer such as Eileen gets, that "all is very, very well." Instead I had a sensation such as a worm might feel if it were ever allowed access to the consciousness of a human being. I was confused and asked the group what answers they had received, and was assured that all would indeed be well (it was). When I shared my own sensation, they looked at me with disbelief and, I think, some disapproval. Evidently, that was not how they experienced their God, which I humbly accepted as evidence of my spiritual immaturity.

That's still true, but I think my different sensation derived not from the usual meditative contact with the Higher Self but from experiencing the Spirit that was accompanying the child's incoming Soul, which is lofty beyond words to express. The same Spirit must have brought me here, and you too, my reader. Such purity must experience this world as pain, which is why we forget that it is there, to spare ourselves the pain. I believe that the atheists and agnostics who are active on behalf of the poor, the homeless, the environment, etc., do so because they are inherently truthful people – they know that a good Omnipotent would have wrought differently – and their truth guides them to the indwelling Spirit and the stark recognition that it is we, not God, who have created Hell on Earth.

Innocence

When Jesus, standing in the garden, saw the torches of the approaching soldiers, he knew that he would face this ordeal alone, but I do not think he realised how lonesome the end would be. The Elohim had withdrawn, as he knew they must. He was just a human soul, though pure and unsullied, but he still clung to the notion of power, saying as he bade Peter put up his sword, "Thinkest thou that I cannot now pray to my Father, and he shall presently give me more than twelve legions of angels." (Mat. 26:53). Then came the successive initiations: the trial; scourging; and nailing to the cross. Crucifixion was essentially a slow death by exhaustion. The victim's body sagged as his strength failed; he could no longer support his weight on his tortured arms and feet; breathing became more and more difficult and he slowly suffocated.

Jesus used the period of dying to accomplish three important tasks. First he forgave the thief on the cross beside him who asked, "Lord, remember me when thou comest into thy kingdom." This thief was Lucifer's representative, and since Jesus was redeeming Lucifer's fault, he had authority to forgive him. Second, he entrusted Mary his mother, representative of Earth, to his disciple John. After the resurrection, Jesus suggests that John will remain here until his return. This must have caused some confusion among the disciples, leading John to remark rather testily that Jesus did not say that he would not die, only that he would tarry here if Jesus so willed. And spiritual lore tells us this is what has happened. We may meet John in the person of Raphael, whose paintings so sublimely celebrate the Blessed Virgin; in the German poet Novalis whose lines achingly evoke his yearning for her wondrous presence, briefly incarnate in his beloved Sophie; and in others through the years. Peter Caddy told of having met him in his current incarnation ass a prominent citizen of Turkey. He remarked, in tones more humble than I ever heard from him, what an experience it was to meet a fully Christed being. St. John leads the path of individual initiation into Christ, as St. Peter leads the corporate path. Unfortunately, as John indicates at the end of his Gospel, Peter was suspicious of him from the beginning, and the churches have persecuted John's followers almost down to the present day

The third task that Jesus accomplished on the cross was to use the extreme pain and exhaustion of crucifixion to prepare his body for resurrection. I have related above how a friend's experience supported the old wisdom, now ridiculed, that pain teaches us to love. We know pain has a purpose on the physical level, where it teaches us to avoid harmful contacts, like fire, and warns us of disease. If it teaches lessons on the physical level, it must teach lessons on the other levels too: "As below, so above," to turn the old tag round. It follows that love may be the lesson on the level of personality. Of course, we may refuse to learn it. That's another saying from *A Course in Miracles*, that free will does not give us the right to decide the curriculum, only how long we take over it.

Steiner tells us that Jesus' physical body was already breaking down, unable to support the intense presence of the Elohim, which was why at the last supper he told Judas Iscariot, "That thou doest, do quickly" (John 13:27), but I believe that resurrection required more work. Jesus made use of his pain and his unconditional love for humanity to spiritualise his body, even altering its physical substance. How else do we explain, except as pointless fabrication, the Gospel story that the soldier's spear let forth a stream of blood and water, unmingled, from the wound? When the change was accomplished, he could allow himself to die. The Elohim may have accompanied him in spirit thus far, but through death they could not go. This was the fiercest initiation. "My God, My God, why hast thou forsaken me?" The Son of Man went through the gate of death alone, ensuring that none of us will ever have to do so, for he will be there to see us safely to the lands beyond.

But that is after we have died. Waiting for death is different. As in a shadow play, we can see that the human race has come by an opposite road to Jesus' same sense of aloneness, for we have forsaken the Truth of God and raised our own idols, religious and secular, in his place. The gap in the ring that I envisioned in Chapter Three has been closed. The circle is complete. And that's OK. We need to be absolute individuals before we are fit to enter God's Kingdom. William Henley expressed the thought succinctly:

Out of the night that covers me
Black as the Pit from pole to pole,
I thank whatever gods may be
For my unconquerable soul.

St. Matthew's Gospel tells that, after the resurrection, there were those among the dead who arose and went into Jerusalem where they appeared to many people. Christian tradition echoes this story, telling that the Son of Man spent the three days in the tomb traversing the levels of Hell, where he released trapped souls. Analogous is the Greek legend of Hercules harrowing Hell, a sun-hero myth that may be precognitive. Traditionally the period between the resurrection and the ascension was forty days, which is scriptural shorthand for a period of medium duration. Forty days was also the time that Jesus spent in the wilderness after the baptism in Jordan, when the Elohim had taken on his flesh. This was the time needed for the Divine to adjust to the conditions of corporality. Similarly, we may see the period between resurrection and ascension as the time needed for the Son of Man to adjust to his new role as Lord of Karma and indwelling Spirit of Earth, wed to her soul, Gaia, whom he had redeemed from the bondage inflicted by millennia of human ill usage. The literal reading of the Gospels, that he was taken up into heaven, which is therefore seen as being in the sky, is a misinterpretation. A more modern understanding informs us that heaven is all around us and is a matter of consciousness rather than place. Ascension means that we rise from the physical level to the levels of soul and spirit, and thereafter are free to take on flesh as we will, for the higher understands the lower, but not vice-versa.

And what of the Elohim? They had fulfilled their karma, and the stories I have heard suggest that they have travelled on the waves of thought, faster than light, to the furthest reaches of the galaxy, taking with them the blessing of the human experience redeemed. They are celebrated in many images and paintings as the Cosmic Christ, that other aspect of our divinity to which we travel. It was not a God that wrought these changes, but Jesus, a human soul, acting in all innocence out of unconditional love, doing in each instant what had to be done. And so became God in truth.

Martyrdom

Petronia was the daughter of a noble Roman family who lived in Carthage during the reign of the Emperor Septimus Severus. Like all the upper classes they were pagan, except for Petronia who had converted to Christianity. Then the Emperor decreed that all Romans must worship him as God or face an unpleasant death. Petronia could easily have saved herself by withdrawing to one of the family's country estates, or simply by staying inside the home until the persecution was over. Her family urged these courses on her, but Petronia was adamant, going regularly to the sacred suppers where bread was broken and wine shared. Summoned before the city magistrate, who was her father's sorrowing friend, Petronia was sentenced to death in the arena, to be torn apart by wild beasts. When the time came, she steadfastly led the small band of her fellow Christians onto the bloodstained sand, with rather unexpected results.

Rome's countless arenas had been capturing animals for so long that they had drained the gene pool of the fiercest, which were the ones most liable to be decoyed into the hunters' nets. Petronia found herself facing a smallish leopard that merely snarled and shied away. The authorities had provided for this eventuality. A soldier stood by with drawn sword, to kill her if the beast refused. But he was young and inexperienced, mourning perhaps for Petronia's youth and resolution. His sword arm drooped. With blazing eyes, Petronia sprang forward, wrested the sword from him and plunged it into her own throat.

In his *History of Western Philosophy*, Bertrand Russell mentions that at one point in the early centuries of the Christian Church, martyrdom became quite popular among its adherents, a sort of short cut to heaven. In fact, bishops had to discourage the faithful from pursuing it, for fear their congregations would be depleted. The message seems to have been lost on Petronia. For all her courage, I think she was just making a statement. If hope of heaven is your motive, your love is transactional and conditional. In the Eastern Orthodox Church she is named a saint, but Roman Catholics only number her among the martyrs.

God as Friend

Jakob Boehme, the German mystic who wrote in the seventeenth century, was called the 'friend of God.' He got into trouble with his Protestant Church, which tends to happen, even today, to anyone laying claim to any special relationship. Although it's not really special. Rather, it is something we can all enjoy if we are willing to open up and experience the simplicity of what is inside us, abandoning the contradictions we have been taught, which require such elaborate justifications. Today the consequences of knowing God as friend are not so dire and many people walk in two worlds like Tolkien's Elves, experiencing the physical and the Beyond together. Neale Donald Walsch's *Conversations with God* is evidence of just such a continuing experience, as is Karin Bogliolo's *In Search of the Magic of Findhorn.*

The connection spans religions. My eldest son has become a Hindu and he delights me with his easy relations with his God, fountain of abundance, love and inspiration. He tells me God is his best friend, and their relationship one of mutual unconditional love. We had been writing each other about it, and that night, he tells me, as he was lying down to sleep and thinking over what he had written, he had the most incredible feeling of warmth right down his back, and the sensation of an arm lying across him: God cuddling up. He went to sleep with a very big smile. Our communication with God can be light-hearted but still serious, a new and quite ideal combination and evidence, I think, of our race's maturation.

Abundance

Peter Caddy taught that God's will for us is Abundance. He demonstrated this through Manifestation, by exemplifying Abundance in his own life. Whole libraries of self-help books tell us how to change our self-consciousness and sense of undeserving and go the same route. They outline a number of methods, but I suggest that when we take God as our friend, we realise that we already have the best and can no longer feel undeserving. Then Abundance becomes a natural outcome of our lives, providing the opportunity to follow our Joy and get creative. Of course, the abundance may not be material. Like

Mother Teresa's, it may be the opportunity to serve, co-creating a sufficiency of funds and helpers. Unconditional love is then a normal state of being and can be offered to all who will accept it. God stands first among the recipients.

Conclusion

What personal qualities did we find in the stories about the givers of unconditional love? We found a rock-like faith and will, which was able to manifest abundance; we found an incredible capacity to endure hardship without faltering; we found the ability to let go; we found innocence; self-sacrifice; service; forgiveness; integrity; spontaneity; constancy; vulnerability; gratitude; purity; joy; loyalty; pain; the ability to heal and transform; and running through them all, strength. We also found unconditional love in the commonplace, in our experience of friends, nature and art.

Such a variety of qualities can only mean this: that unconditional love is present in all of us, waiting only to be summoned into consciousness. Imagine that we are like cells in the human body, but each of us conscious of the whole and each with a role that is essential to it. If we get egotistical we become cancerous, but if we live in unconditional love we serve both the whole and ourselves, seeing the Christ in the other.

*Exercises*

*Read over the qualities of unconditional love listed above. Is there one you feel drawn to? One that would help you grow? Or do you spot one that was missed from the list? Whichever one you are drawn to, ask how you may use it in service to the planet. Then, if it still seems right to you, go into the Silence and ask for the quality, and for the strength to use it. Then rest peacefully.*

*Write down your experience. Afterwards, take time to review all that you have written in your journal. Then go into the Silence and ask where next your life should take you.*

# BIBLIOGRAPHY

Anonymous, *A Course in Miracles*, Foundation for Inner Peace, Mill Valley, CA 1975

Apuleius, Lucius, *The Golden Ass*, trans. P.G Walsh, OUP 1995

Beauvoir, Simone de, *The Second Sex*, Random House, NY 1990

*Bhagavad Gita,* translated by Charles Johnston, Theosophical Society, NY 1906

Bogliolo, Karin and Newfeld, Carly, *In Search of the Magic of Findhorn*, Findhorn Press 2002

Caddy, Peter, *In Perfect Timing*, Findhorn Press 1996

Caddy, Eileen, *Flight into Freedom and Beyond*, Findhorn Press 2002

*God Spoke to Me*, Findhorn Press 1992

*Opening Doors Within*, Findhorn Press 1987

*Loving Unconditionally* audio-tape, Findhorn Press 1981

Cooper, Diana, *A Little Light on Angels*, Findhorn Press 1996

David-Neel, Alexandra, *Initiations and Initiates in Tibet*, Dover NY 1993

*Magic and Mystery in Tibet*, Dover NY 1971

Dubois, Marianne, *Solar Encounters*, Hazelwood Press, Devon UK 1996

Eide, Rita, *The Celestial Voice of Diana*, Findhorn Press 1999

Findhorn Community, The, *The Findhorn Garden*, HarperCollins 1976

Fromm, Erich, *The Art of Loving*, HarperCollins, 1956

Grant, Joan, *Winged Pharaoh*, Ariel, Georgia 1985

Graves, Robert, *The White Goddess*, Faber, London 1962

Grimble, Arthur, *A Pattern of Islands*, John Murray, London 1952

*Return to the Islands*, John Murray, London 1960

Hall, Judy, *The Art of Psychic Protection*, Findhorn Press 1996

*Deja Who?*, Findhorn Press 1998

Johnson, Raynor, *The Imprisoned Splendour*, Harper & Row, NY 1953
Lao-Tsu, *The Way and Its Power*, trans. Arthur Waley, Grove Press NY 1988
Main, Darren John, *The Findhorn Book of Meditation*, Findhorn Press 2003
Moyne, John and Barks, Coleman, *Versions of Rumi*, Threshold Books, VT 1984
Mutwa, Credo, *Indaba My Children*, Blue Crane Books, Johannesburg 1963
Pearsall, Paul, *The Heart's Code*, Thorson, NY 1998
Pogacnik, Marko, *Nature Spirits and Elemental Beings*, Findhorn Press 1997
*Christ Power and the Earth Goddess*, Findhorn Press 1999
*Earth Changes, Human Destiny*, Findhorn Press 2000
*Daughter of Gaia*, Findhorn Press 2001
Powell S.J., John, *Unconditional Love*, Thomas More, Allen TX 1999
Remen, Rachel Naomi M.D., *Kitchen Table Wisdom*, Riverhead Books, Putnam NY 1996
Sayers, Dorothy L., *The Man Born to be King*, Ignatius Press, San Francisco 1990
Spangler, David, *A Pilgrim in Aquarius*, Findhorn Press 1996
Steiner, Rudolf, *From Jesus to Christ*, Rudolf Steiner Press, Sussex, England 1991
*Gospel of St. John*, Anthroposophic Press, NY 1962
*Gospel of St. John and Its Relation to the Other Gospels*, Anthroposophic Press, NY 1982
*Gospel of St. Luke*, Rudolf Steiner Press, London 1964
*Gospel of St. Mark*, Anthroposophic Press, NY 1986
*Gospel of St. Matthew*, Rudolf Steiner Press, London 1965
*The Fifth Gospel*, Rudolf Steiner Press, Sussex, England 1995
Twyman, James F., *The Secret of the Beloved Disciple*, Findhorn Press 2000
*Portrait of the Master*, Findhorn Press 2000
*Praying Peace*, Findhorn Press 2000
Van der Post, Laurens, *The Heart of the Hunter*, Harcourt & Brace, NY 1980
Van Lippe-Biesterfeld, Irene, *Dialogue with Nature*, Findhorn Press 1997
Walsch, Neale Donald, *Conversations with God*, Putnam, NY 1996